ADULT ONLY

OFFICE JOKES

Guaranteed to make you giggle!

HB

HINKLER
BOOKS

Joke Compilation: Scribblers and Writers
Cover Design: Sam Grimmer
Illustrations: John Shakespeare
Editor: Jasmine Chan
Typesetting: Midland Typesetters, Maryborough, Vic, Australia

Adults Only Office Jokes
First published in 2004 by Hinkler Books Pty Ltd
17-23 Redwood Drive
Dingley Victoria 3172 Australia
www.hinklerbooks.com.au

First printed in 2004
Reprinted 2005

ISBN 1 7412 1659 1

Printed and bound in Australia

INTRODUCTION

The office is a great place to . . . do everything but work! You can drink coffee, snooze, crack jokes, wander around aimlessly or endeavour to develop a romance.

You can send up the management, bring down the business or send people spinning sideways.

The office is the place of bureaucracy gone mad, memos of power, notices of threat and e-mails of angst.

People come and go, careers rocket and burn, minds are numbed and bodies are wrecked.

Love blossoms and fades, tempers flare, rivalries develop and mateship is formed.

And the burning fire of jealousy lingers forever . . .

In an enthralling atmosphere like this, a crazy humour emerges. Jokes, pranks, e-mails and bogus memos satirise the madness of it all.

We have captured it all here in this book.

The highs and lows, tears and cheers, victories and defeats and above all, the laughs of spending five days a week in an office, wondering why the heck you are there, other than the fact that you have to eat and pay rent. Oh and there's a movie you might like to see at the weekend. And what about that lovely jacket you saw in the window only yesterday . . .?

Enjoy it.

Then get back to work . . . the boss is coming.

AH-HA! SO, THAT'S HOW PEOPLE DO 'IT'

How lawyers do it . . .
Lawyers do it with appeal.
Lawyers do it confidentially.
Lawyers do it on a trial basis.
Lawyers do it as long as you can pay them.

How accountants do it . . .

Accountants do it by the book.
Accountants do it with double entries.
Accountants are Certified to do it in Public.
Accountants do it without losing their balance.
Accountants do it within budget.

How economists do it . . .

Economists do it cyclically.
Economists do it on demand.
Economists do it with models.
Economists advise Presidents how to do it.

How merchants do it . . .

Merchants do it to customers.
Merchants do it in gift wraps.
Merchants do it in a job lot.

How journalists do it . . .
Journalists do it on the front page.
Journalists do it with special editions.
Journalists do it with cameras and tape recorders.

How bankers do it . . .

Bankers do it risk-free.
Bankers charge a fee each time they do it.
Bankers do it with varying rates of interest.
Bankers do it with a penalty for early withdrawal.

How philosophers do it . . .

Philosophers do it deeper.
Philosophers do it conceptually.
Philosophers think about doing it.
Philosophers wonder why they did it.

How teachers do it . . .

Teachers do it with class.
Teachers make you do it till you get it right.
Teachers spend all weekend writing reports about it.

How musicians do it . . .

Musicians do it with rhythm.
Musicians do it in quartets.
Musicians do it according to the conductor's instructions.
Jazz musicians do it with improvisations.
Band members do it in front of 10,000 people.
Rock drummers do it after driving the Rolls Royce into the
  hotel pool.
Lead guitarists do it solo.
Lead singers can't remember doing it.
Bass players do it, but no-one notices.

How firemen do it . . .

Firemen do it wearing rubber.
Firemen do it with a big hose.
Firemen do it with a lot of heat.
Firemen find them hot and leave them wet.
Firemen do it without taking their hats off.

How artists do it . . .

Artists do it by design.
Artists do it with creativity.
Artists do it with flair.
Artists do it with longer strokes.

How bartenders do it . . .

Bartenders do it on the rocks.
Bartenders do it as you wish.
Bartenders do it for tips.

How cops do it . . .

Cops do it by the book.
Cops do it with handcuffs.
Detectives do it under cover.
Uniform men do it without a break for 12 hours.

How biologists do it . . .

Biologists do it with clones.
Botanists do it in the bushes.
Zoologists do it with animals.

How pharmacists do it . . .

Pharmacists do it with drugs.
Pharmacists do it by prescription.
Pharmacists do it with side effects.
Pharmacists do it over the counter.

How statisticians do it . . .

Statisticians probably do it.
Statisticians do it continuously but discretely.
Statisticians do it with large numbers.
Statisticians do it. After all, it's only normal.
Statisticians do it with standard deviations.

How actuaries do it . . .

Actuaries do it without risk.
Actuaries do it with frequency and severity.
Actuaries do it until death or disability, whichever comes first.

How insurance agents do it . . .

Insurance agents are premium lovers.
Insurance agents do it with third parties.
Insurance agencies will only do it under the provisions written
in very tiny type at the bottom of the policy.

How advertisers do it . . .

Advertisers do it publicly.
Advertisers do it with a lot of noise.
Advertisers do it within thirty seconds.
Advertisers do it with promises to be the best.

How advertising agency executives do it . . .

Ad executives do it only after a white-board, round-table brain-
storm.
Ad executives do it after all the survey data has been analysed.
After it's done, ad executives send it down to Creative.

How physicists do it . . .

Physicists do it at the speed of light.
Physicists understand the theory of how to do it, but have
difficulty obtaining practical results.
Physicists compute the likely outcome on the basis of data
available.
Physicists do it with a Big Bang.

How aerodynamicists do it . . .

Aerodynamicists do it in drag.
Aerodynamicists like to do it on the wing.

Aerodynamicists have a fascination with the cock-pit.

How psychiatrists do it . . .

Psychiatrists do it on the couch.
Psychiatrists think they do it.
Psychiatrists do it for at least 50 dollars per session.
Psychiatrists ask you about your relationship with your mother
before doing it.

How astronomers do it . . .

Astronomers do it all night.
Astronomers do it over extremely long distances . . .
Astronomers like to go on for several million light years.
Astronomers do it with white dwarfs and red giants.

How chemists do it . . .

Chemists do it reactively.
Chemists do it in an excited state.

Chemists do it periodically on the table.
Polymer chemists do it in chains.
Pharmaceutical chemists do it with drugs.
Analytical chemists do it with precision and accuracy.

How engineers do it . . .

Engineers do it with precision.
Electrical engineers do it on an impulse.
Electrical engineers do it with more frequency and less resistance.
Mechanical engineers do it with stress and strain.
City planners do it with their eyes closed.
Petroleum engineers do it with lubrication.
Reservoir engineers do it thoroughly and with a lot of simulation.

How social workers do it . . .

Social workers do it for the community.
Social workers do it with a lot of paperwork.
Social workers don't do it; they just share the experience.
Social workers describe even their most intimate partners as
    'clients'.
At the end, a social worker will ask, 'How are you feeling?'

How dentists do it . . .

Dentists do it orally.
Dentists do it with drills and on chairs.
Dentists like to take pictures.
Dentists love to have someone else in the room.
Dentists can't do it in the dark.
Dentists will do it on a bridge, across a canal or over a plate.
Dentists do it and then tell you to spit.

ASTROLOGICAL BUSINESS SIGNS . . .

Marketing

You are ambitious, yet stupid. You chose a marketing degree to avoid having to study in college, concentrating instead on drinking and socialising. Fortunately, this is pretty much what your job responsibilities are now. Least compatible with Sales.

Sales

Laziest of all signs and is often referred to as 'marketing without a degree'. You are self centred and paranoid. Unless someone calls you and begs you to take their money, you like to avoid contact with customers so you can 'concentrate on the big picture'. You seek admiration for your golf game throughout your life.

Information Technology

Unable to control anything in your personal life, you are instead content to completely control everything that happens at your workplace. Often even you don't understand what you are saying but who the hell can tell. It is written that Geeks shall inherit the Earth.

Human Resources

Ironically, given your access to confidential information, you tend to be the biggest gossip within the organisation. Possibly the only other person that does less work than marketing, you are unable to return any calls today because you have to get a haircut, have lunch and then mail a letter.

Middle Management

Catty, cut-throat and yet completely spineless, you are destined to remain at your current job for the rest of your life. Unable to make a single decision, you tend to measure your worth by the number of meetings you can schedule for yourself. Best suited to marry other 'Middle Managers' as everyone in your social circle is a 'Middle Manager'.

Senior Management

(See above—Same sign, different title)

Customer Service

Bright, cheery, positive, you are a 50 cent cab ride from taking your own life. As children none of you asked your parents for a little cubicle and a headset so you could pretend to play 'Customer Service'. Continually passed over for promotions, your best bet is to sleep with your manager.

Consultant

Lacking any specific knowledge you use acronyms to avoid revealing your utter lack of experience. You have convinced yourself that your 'skills' are in demand and that you could get a higher paying job with any other organisation in a heartbeat. You will spend an eternity contemplating these career opportunities without ever taking direct action.

Recruiter/Head-hunter

As a person that profits from the success of others, most people who actually work for a living disdain you. Paid on commission and susceptible to alcoholism, your ulcers and frequent heart attacks correspond directly with fluctuations in the stock market.

Partner, President or CEO

You are brilliant or lucky. Your inability to figure out complex systems such as the fax machine suggest the latter.

Government Worker

Government workers are genius inventors, like the invention of new holidays. You usually suffer from deep depression or anxiety and usually commit serious crimes while on the job. You are most productive when on sick leave.

A customer sent an order to a distributor for a large amount of goods.

The distributor noticed that the previous bill hadn't been paid, so he rang and left a voicemail message for them saying, 'We can't ship your new order until you pay for the last one.'

The next day the distributor received a collect phone call, 'Please cancel the order. We can't wait that long.'

A woman desperately looking for work went into a factory. The personnel manager looked over her resume and regretfully explained to her that he had nothing worthy of her talents.

The woman answered that she really needed work and would take almost anything.

The personnel manager hummed and hah-ed and finally said that he did have a low-skill job on the Tickle Me Elmo line, but nothing else.

The woman happily accepted his offer. He took her down to the line, explained her duties and told her to report at 8 am the next day.

The next day at 8.45 there was a knock at the personnel manager's door.

The Tickle Me Elmo line manager came in and started ranting about the woman who had just been hired.

He demanded that the personnel manager come down to see the problem.

Together they went down to the line where there was a huge back-log of Elmos. The newly hired woman was right in the middle of them.

They watched, intrigued, as she cut a little piece of fabric from the huge roll of Elmo fur. She also had a big bag of marbles. She took two marbles and a square of fur and started sewing them between Elmo's legs.

The personnel manager started laughing uncontrollably.

Finally, he pulled himself together, walked over to the new employee and said, 'I'm sorry. I guess you misunderstood me yesterday. 'What I wanted you to do was give Elmo two test tickles . . .'

A guy went to apply for a job with the US Postal Service. During the interview, the interviewer asked the guy if he was a veteran.

The guy said 'Yes, I fought over in Vietnam.'

Then the interviewer asked if the guy had any disabilities.

The guy responded, 'Well, I stepped on a landmine over there and blew my testicles off.'

'Great!' the interviewer responded. 'We give disabled vets preference. You can start tomorrow morning at 10 am.'

'But doesn't everyone normally start at 8 am?' asked the guy.

'Yes, but you don't have to come in until 10. All we do is just stand around and scratch our balls for the first two hours anyway.'

A new manager spends a week at his new office with the manager he is replacing.

On the last day the departing manager tells him, 'I have left three numbered envelopes in the desk drawer.

'Open an envelope if you encounter a crisis you can't solve.'

Three months down the track everything goes horribly wrong. The manager starts to panic but then he remembers the three envelopes in his drawer.

He opens the envelope numbered one.

The message inside says 'Blame your predecessor!'

He does this and gets off the hook.

About six months later, the company experiences a dip in sales combined with serious product problems.

The manager cracks open the second envelope.

The message reads, 'Reorganise!'

This he does and the company quickly rebounds.

Three months later, beset by another crisis, the manager opens the third envelope.

The message inside says, 'Prepare three envelopes'.

THAT'S ... WHAT IT'S ALL ABOUT

You see a gorgeous girl at a party. You go up to her and say, 'I'm fantastic in bed.'

That's Direct Marketing.

You're at a party with a bunch of friends and see a gorgeous girl. One of your friends goes up to her and pointing at you says, 'He's fantastic in bed.'

That's Advertising.

You see a gorgeous girl at a party. You go up to her and get her telephone number. The next day you call and say, 'Hi, I'm fantastic in bed.'

That's Telemarketing.

You're at a party and see a gorgeous girl. You get up and straighten your tie, you walk up to her and pour her a drink. You open the door for her, pick up her bag after she drops it, offer her a ride and then say, 'By the way, I'm fantastic in bed.'

That's Public Relations.

You're at a party and see a gorgeous girl. She walks up to you and says, 'I hear you're fantastic in bed.'

That's Brand Recognition.

A real estate salesman had just closed his first deal, only to discover that the piece of land he had sold was completely under water.

'That customer's going to come back here pretty mad,' he said to his boss. 'Should I give him his money back?'

'Money back?' roared the boss. 'What kind of salesman are you? Get out there and sell him a houseboat.'

The boss came early in the morning one day and found his manager screwing his secretary.

He shouted at him, 'Is this what I pay you for?'

The manager replied, 'No, sir, this I do free of charge.'

Five cannibals are appointed as engineers in a defence company. During the welcoming ceremony the boss says, 'You're all part of our team now. You can earn good money here and anytime you want, you can go to the cafeteria for something to eat. So please don't trouble any of the other employees.'

The cannibals promised to leave the employees alone.

Four weeks later the boss returns and says, 'You're all working very hard and I'm very satisfied with all of you.

'However, one of our janitors has disappeared. Do any of you know what happened to him?'

The cannibals all shake their heads and mumble no.

After the boss has left, the leader of the cannibals says to the others, 'Which of you idiots ate the janitor?'

A hand raises hesitantly, to which the leader of the cannibals replies, 'You fool! For four weeks we've been eating Team Leaders, Supervisors and Project Managers and no one noticed anything and you have to go and eat the cleaner!'

When Joe's wife left him he got so depressed that his doctor sent him to see a psychiatrist.

Joe told the psychiatrist his troubles and said, 'Life isn't worth living.'

'Don't be stupid, Joe,' said the psychiatrist. 'Let work be your salvation. I want you to totally submerge yourself in your work. Now, what do you do for a living?'

'I clean out septic tanks,' Joe replied.

An applicant was filling out a job application. When he came to the question, 'Have you ever been arrested?' he wrote, 'No.'

The next question, intended for people who had answered in the affirmative to the previous question, was 'Why?'

The applicant answered it anyway, 'Never got caught.'

A guy works at a new job on Thursday and Friday. On Monday he calls in and says, 'I can't come in today. I'm sick.'

He worked the rest of the week, but the following Monday he calls in and says, 'I can't come in today. I'm sick.'

The boss asks the foreman about him and the foreman says, 'He's great. He does the work of two men. We need him.'

So the boss calls the guy into his office and says, 'You seem to have a problem getting to work on Mondays. You're a good worker and I'd hate to fire you. What's the problem? Anything we can help you with? Drugs? Alcohol?'

The guy says, 'No, I don't drink or do drugs. But my brother-in-law drinks every weekend and then beats on my sister. So every Monday morning, I go over to make sure she's all right. She puts her head on my shoulder and cries, one thing leads to another and the next thing you know, I'm screwing her.'

The boss says, 'You screw your sister?'

The guy says, 'Hey, I told you I was sick.'

A bank manager was down to the final two candidates for one cashier's position.

The first one interviewed was from a small college in upstate New York. A nice young man, but a bit timid.

Then he called for the second man, 'Jim Johnson!'

Up stepped a burly young man who seemed quite sure of himself.

'He looks like he can take care of any situation,' thought the manager and decided, there and then, to hire him.

Turning to Johnson, he said, 'Now Jim, I like the way you carry yourself—that's an important asset for the job as cashier. However, you must be precise. I noticed you did not fill out the place on the application where we asked your formal education.'

Jim looked a little confused so the manager said, 'Where did you get your financial education?'

'Oh,' replied Jim, 'Yale.'

'That's very good . . . excellent. You're hired!'

'Now that you're working for us, what do you prefer to be called?'

Jim answered 'I don't care . . . Yim . . . or Mr Yonson.'

All the organs of the body were having a meeting, trying to decide who was in charge.

The brain said, 'I should be in charge, because I run all the body's systems, so without me nothing would happen.'

'I should be in charge,' said the heart, 'Because I pump the blood and circulate oxygen all over the body, so without me you'd all waste away.'

'I should be in charge,' said the stomach, 'Because I process food and give all of you energy.'

'I should be in charge,' said the rectum, 'Because I'm responsible for waste removal.'

All the other body parts laughed at the rectum and insulted him, so in a huff, he shut down.

Within a few days, the brain had a terrible headache, the stomach was bloated and the blood was toxic. Eventually the other organs gave in. They all agreed that the rectum should be the boss.

The moral of the story?

You don't have to be smart or important to be in charge . . . just an asshole.

An office manager had money problems and had to fire an employee, either Jack or Jill. He thought he'd fire the employee who came to work late.

The next morning, both employees came to work very early.

So the manager thought he would fire the first one who took a coffee break. Unfortunately, neither employee took a coffee break.

Then the manager decided to see who took the longest lunch break. Strangely, neither Jack nor Jill took a lunch break that day. They both ate at their desk.

Then the manager thought he'd wait to see who would leave work earliest, but both employees stayed after closing.

Jill finally went to the coat rack and the manager went up to her and said, 'Jill, I have a terrible problem. I don't know whether to lay you or Jack off.'

Jill said, 'Well, you'd better jack off, because I'm late for my bus.'

Tom had this problem of getting up at the right time in the morning and was always late for work.

His boss was mad at him and threatened to fire him if he didn't do something about it.

So Tom went to his doctor who gave him a pill and told him to take it before he went to bed.

Tom slept well and in fact beat the alarm in the morning. He had a leisurely breakfast and drove cheerfully to work. 'Boss,' he said, 'The pill actually worked!'

'That's all fine,' said the boss. 'But where were you yesterday?'

Down on her luck, Julie the blonde decides to go to the swish part of town and earn some extra money doing some handyman jobs.

At the first house she comes to she rings the doorbell and asks if there are any odd jobs she could do.

'Well, actually,' the man replied, 'We need the porch painted. How much would you charge?'

Julie said she felt $50 was fair.

'Okay. The ladders, paint and other tools you need are in the garage,' he replied. When the man closed the door, his wife who had overheard the conversation, asked him, '$50?? Does she realise that the porch goes all the way around the house?'

The man replied, 'She must have, she was standing right on it.'

About 45 minutes later the doorbell rings again and the man is surprised to find Julie there.

She tells him that she's done and says that she even had enough paint to do two coats. As the man is reaching into his wallet to pay her, Julie says, 'Oh and by the way, that isn't a Porsche—it's a Ferrari.'

Three blondes were all vying for the last available position on the local police force.

The detective conducting the interview looked at the three of them and said, 'So you all want to be a cop, eh?'

The blondes all nodded. The detective got up, opened a file drawer and pulled out a file folder.

Sitting back down, he opened it up and withdrew a photograph and said, 'To be a detective, you have to be able to detect. You must be able to notice things such as distinguishing features and oddities such as scars and so on.'

He stuck the photo right in the face of the first blonde and withdrew it after just two seconds.

'Now' he said, 'Did you notice any distinguishing features about this man?'

The blonde immediately said, 'Yes, I did. He only has one eye!'

The detective shook his head and said, 'Of course he only has one eye in this picture! It's a profile of his face! You're dismissed!'

The first blonde hung her head and walked out of the office.

The detective then turned to the second blonde, stuck the photo in her face for two seconds, pulled it back and said, 'What about you? Notice anything unusual or outstanding about this man?'

The blonde immediately shot back, 'Yep! He only has one ear!'

The detective put his head in his hand and exclaimed, 'Didn't you hear what I just said to the other lady?

'This is a profile of the man's face! Of course you can only see one ear! You're excused, too! You'd never make a good detective!'

The second blonde sheepishly walked out of the office.

The detective turned his attention to the last blonde and said, 'This is probably a waste of time, but . . .'

He flashed the photo in her face for a couple of seconds and withdrew it, saying, 'Alright. Did you notice anything distinguishing or unusual about this man?'

The blonde said, 'Yes, I did. This man wears contact lenses.'

The detective frowned, took another look at the picture and began looking at some of the papers in the folder.

He looked up at the blonde with a puzzled expression and said, 'You're absolutely right!

'His bio says he wears contacts! How in the world could you tell that by looking at this picture?'

The blonde rolled her eyes and said, 'Duh! He has only one eye and one ear, he certainly can't wear glasses!'

Two telephone company crews were putting up telephone poles. At the end of the day, the company foreman asked the first crew how many poles they had put in the ground. Fifteen was the answer.

'Not bad, not bad at all,' the foreman said.

Turning to the blonde crew he asked how many they had put in. 'Four' was the reply.

'Four?' the foreman yelled. 'The others did 15 and you only did four?'

'Yes,' replied the leader of the blonde group, 'But look at how much they left sticking out of the ground.'

AT THE COAL-FACE . . .

It was the first day of John's new job at a large firm. The manager invited him into his office for a chat.

'What is your name?' was the first thing the manager asked.

'John,' the new guy replied.

The manager scowled, 'Look, I don't know what kind of a namby-pamby place you worked at before, but I don't call anyone by their first name. It breeds familiarity and that leads to a breakdown in authority. I refer to my employees by their last name only—Smith, Jones, Baker—that's all. I am to be referred to only as Robertson. Now that we have got that straight, what is your last name?'

John sighed and said, 'Darling. My name is John Darling.'

'Okay, John, the next thing I want to tell you is . . .'

A DAY OFF?

So you want the day off? Let's take a look at what you are asking for . . .

- There are 365 days per year available for work.
- There are 52 weeks per year in which you already have 2 days off per week, leaving 261 days available for work.
- Since you spend 16 hours each day away from work, you have used up 170 days, leaving only 91 days available.
- You spend 30 minutes each day on coffee break. That accounts for 23 days each year, leaving only 68 days available.
- With a one hour lunch period each day, you have used up another 46 days, leaving only 22 days available for work.
- You normally spend 2 days per year on sick leave. This leaves

you only 20 days available for work.
- We are off for 5 public holidays per year, so your available working time is down to 15 days.
- We generously give you 14 days vacation per year.

That leaves only 1 day available for work and I'll be damned if you're going to take that day off!

SAYINGS THAT SHOULD BE ON THOSE OFFICE INSPIRATIONAL POSTERS . . .

- If you can stay calm, while all around you is chaos, then you probably haven't completely understood the seriousness of the situation.
- Doing a job right the first time gets the job done. Doing the job wrong 14 times gives you job security.
- Eagles may soar, but weasels don't get sucked into jet engines.
- Artificial Intelligence is no match for Natural Stupidity.
- A person who smiles in the face of adversity probably has a scapegoat.
- Plagiarism saves time.

- If at first you don't succeed, try management.
- Never put off until tomorrow what you can avoid altogether.
- Teamwork . . . means never having to take all the blame yourself.
- Never underestimate the power of very stupid people in large groups.
- Hang in there, retirement is only 30 years away!
- Go the extra mile. It makes your boss look like an incompetent slacker.
- When the going gets tough, the tough take a coffee break.
- Indecision is the key to Flexibility.
- Aim low, reach your goals, avoid disappointment.
- Rome did not create a great empire by having meetings, they did it by killing all.

THE WORKERS' PRAYER

Grant me the serenity to accept the things I cannot change. The courage to change the things I cannot accept.

And the wisdom to hide the bodies of those people I had to kill today because they pissed me off.

TEN REASONS PEOPLE SHOULD BE DRUNK AT THE WORKPLACE . . .

1. It leads to more communication.
2. It makes fellow employees look better.
3. It cuts down on time off because you can work with a hangover.
4. Employees tell management what they think, not what management wants to hear.
5. It increases job satisfaction because if you have a bad job, you don't realise it.
6. It eliminates vacations because people would rather come to work.
7. It reduces complaints about low pay.
8. It promotes honesty.
9. Bosses are more likely to hand out raises when they are wasted.
10. Suddenly, farting during a meeting isn't so embarrassing.

PRISON AND WORK

In prison: You spend the majority of your time in an 8 x 10 cell.
At work: You spend most of your time in a 6 x 8 cubicle.

In prison: You get three free meals a day.
At work: You get a break for one meal and you have to pay for it.

In prison: You get time off for good behaviour.
At work: You get rewarded for good behaviour with more work.

In prison: A guard locks and unlocks all the doors for you.
At work: You must carry around a security card and unlock and open all the doors yourself.

In prison: All expenses are paid by taxpayers with no work
required.
At work:　You get to pay all the expenses to go to work and then
they deduct taxes from your salary to pay for
prisoners.

In prison: You spend most of your life looking through bars from
inside wanting to get out.
At work:　You spend most of your time wanting to get out and
go inside bars.

In prison: There are wardens who are often sadistic.
At work: They are called supervisors.

A man walks into a bar and orders a beer. The bartender charges
him 15 cents. Confused but not complaining, the man pays.

After a while, he decides to have another beer and some food,
so he orders another beer and a steak. The bartender charges him
50 cents: 15 for the beer and 35 for the food.

After finishing his food and drink, he calls the bartender over
and says, 'Mate, that was the best steak I've ever had. I want to talk
to the manager and thank him.'

'No problem,' says the bartender. 'He's upstairs with my wife.'

'What's he doing upstairs with your wife?' asks the man.

'Probably the same thing I'm doing to his business down here!'

An enthusiastic door-to-door vacuum salesman goes to the first
house in his new territory.

He knocks on the door and a really tough looking lady opens
the door.

Before she has a chance to say anything, he runs inside and
dumps cow pats all over the carpet.

He says, 'Lady, if this vacuum cleaner doesn't clean this up, I'll
eat every chunk of it.'

She turns to him with a smirk and says, 'Do you want tomato sauce with that?'

The salesman says, 'Why do you ask?'

She says, 'We have just moved in and we haven't got the electricity turned on yet.'

BANKERS

If you owe the bank $100, that's your problem. If you owe the bank $100 million, that's the bank's frigging problem.

A young banker decided to buy his first tailor made suit. He went to the finest tailor in town and was measured for a suit.

A week later he went in for his first fitting. He put on the suit and he looked fantastic—he knew he could do some serious deals in this suit.

As he was preening himself in front of the mirror he reached down to put his hands in the pockets and to his surprise he noticed that there were no pockets.

He mentioned this to the tailor who asked him, 'Didn't you tell me you were a banker?'

The young man answered, 'Yes, I did.'

To this the tailor said, 'Who ever heard of a banker with his hands in his own pockets?'

A man walks into a New York City bank and says he wants to borrow $2000 for three weeks.

The loan officer asks him what kind of collateral he has.

The man says 'I've got a Rolls Royce, keep it until the loan is paid off, here are the keys.'

The loan officer promptly has the car driven into the bank's underground parking for safe keeping and gives the man $2000.

Three weeks later the man comes into the bank, pays back the $2000 loan, plus $10 interest and regains possession of the Rolls Royce.

The loan officer asks him, 'Sir, if I may ask, why would a man who drives a Rolls Royce need to borrow $2000 dollars?'

The man answers, 'I had to go to Europe for three weeks and where else could I store a Roller for that long for ten dollars?'

CRASHING COMPUTERS

The Three Laws of Secure Computing

1. Don't buy a computer.
2. If you do buy a computer, don't plug it in.
3. If you do plug it in, sell it and return to step one.

COMPUTERS AND MEN AND WOMEN

Computers are like men . . .

- In order to get their attention, you have to turn them on.
- They are supposed to help you solve problems, but half the time they are the problem.
- They have a lot of data but are still clueless.
- As soon as you commit to one, you realise that, if you had waited a little longer you could have had a better model.
- They hear what you say, but not what you mean.

Computers are like women . . .

- No one but the Creator understands their internal logic.
- The native language they use to communicate with other computers is incomprehensible to everyone else.
- Even your smallest mistakes are stored in long-term memory for later retrieval.
- As soon as you make a commitment to one, you find yourself spending half your pay-cheque on accessories for it.
- You do the same thing for years and suddenly it's wrong.

Real users

- Real users find the one combination of bizarre input values that shuts down the system for days.
- Real users never know what they want, but they always know when your program doesn't deliver it.
- Real users never use the Help key.
- Real users never stop asking for new options.
- Real users never know what to do with new options.

IF COMPUTER ERRORS WERE WRITTEN AS HAIKUS

Three things are certain:
Death, taxes and lost data.
Guess which has occurred.

The file you need
Might be very useful.
But now it is gone.

Windows NT crashed.
I am the Blue Screen of Death.
No one hears your screams.

Yesterday it worked.
Today it is not working.
Windows is like that.

Chaos reigns within.
Reflect, repent, reboot.
Order shall return.

With searching comes loss
And the presence of absence:

File not found.
The Web site you seek
Cannot be located but
Endless others exist.

You step in the stream,
But the water has moved on.
This page is not here.

Stay the patient course.
Of little worth is your ire.
The network is down.

First snow, then silence.
This thousand dollar screen dies
So beautifully.

Printer not ready.
Could be a fatal error.
Have a pen handy?

THE SEVEN TYPES OF INFORMATION TECHNOLOGY SUPPORT STAFF

1. The Know-it-All: 'Well, I could tell you how to do it that way . . . but I think I could recommend a better approach . . .'
2. The New Kid: 'What's my name? I'll have to get back to you on that.'
3. The Psycho: 'Read my lips, bozo! Are you stupid or something?! You can't do that!'
4. The Counsellor: 'Oh my. Oh dear. Uh huh . . . yes . . . and then what happened? . . . Yes, I have plenty of time . . . oh, no, no problem, that's my job . . .'
5. The Intimidator: 'Why did you do THAT?! Haven't you had any training?! Don't you know Section 5.1.2.1.1 of the IEEE spec?'

6. The Veteran: 'Oh! That's there for backward compatibility. They added it in rev 2.00.03 but they didn't document it.'
7. The Crispy Critter: 'I don't know. I don't care. Your problem, that says it all, I have my own to take care of. Why are you using this product, anyway?'

To err . . .
  To err is human . . .
  To err is human; to blame your computer for your mistakes is even more human.
  To err is human; to really foul things up requires a computer.
  Computers are unreliable, but humans are even more unreliable.

A computer help desk operator took a call from a baffled user. 'I am having trouble starting up my computer . . .'
  'Well what seems to be the problem?' asked the help desk.
  'It says to 'Press Any Key'. The problem is I can't find the 'Any' key on the keyboard.'

COMPUTER PROBLEM QUESTIONNAIRE

Describe your problem.

Now, describe the problem accurately.

Speculate wildly about the cause of the problem.

Is your computer plugged in?

Is it turned on?

Have you tried to fix it yourself?

Have you made it worse?

Have you read the manual?

Are you sure you've read the manual?

Are you absolutely certain you've read the manual?

Do you think you understood it?

If 'Yes', then why can't you fix the problem yourself?

What were you doing with your computer at the time the problem occurred?

If 'nothing', then explain why you were logged in.

Are you sure you aren't imagining the problem?

Do you have any independent witnesses of the problem?

Can't you do something else, instead of bothering me?

TOP EXPLANATIONS BY PROGRAMMERS

Strange . . . I've never heard about that.

It did work yesterday.

How is this possible?

The machine seems to have a malfunction.

The user has made an error again.

There is something wrong in your data.

It's just some unlucky coincidence.

This can't do that!

Didn't I fix it already?

This time it will surely run.

According to my calculations the problem doesn't exist.

WHAT COMPUTER MESSAGES REALLY MEAN . . .

Press Any Key.
(Press any key you like, sucker, but I'm not moving.)

Fatal Error. Please contact technical support quoting error no.
1A4-2546512430E . . .
(You will be kept on hold for 10 minutes, only to be told that it's a hardware problem.)

Installing program to C:\ . . .
(I'll also be writing a few files into c:\windows and c:\windows\system where you'll never find them.)

Not enough memory.
(I don't care if you've got 64 MB of RAM, I want to use the bit below 640K.)

Cannot read from drive D:\ . . .
(However, if you put the CD in right side up . . .)

Please Wait . . .
(Indefinitely.)

Directory does not exist . . .
(Any more. Whoops.)

The application caused an error. Choose Ignore or Close. (Makes no difference to me, you're still not getting your work back.)

SEVEN THINGS YOU DON'T WANT TO HEAR YOUR SYSTEM ADMINISTRATOR SAYING:

1. No! Not that button!
2. Do you smell something?
3. I have never seen it do that before . . .
4. The drive ate the tape but that's okay, I brought my screwdriver.
5. Oops. I hope you saved your work.
6. What do you mean you needed that directory?
7. Where did you say those backup tapes were kept?

A DAY AT THE OFFICE

After a hard day at the office, Norman exclaimed, 'I'd give a thousand dollars to the man who would worry for me!'

Bill replied, 'You're on. Now, where are those thousand dollars?' That is your first worry!'

A worker who was being paid weekly approached his employer and held up his last pay-cheque.

'This is 200 dollars less than we agreed on,' he said.

'I know,' the employer said. 'But last week I overpaid you 200 dollars and you never complained.'

'Well, I don't mind an occasional mistake,' the worker answered, 'But when it gets to be a habit, I feel I have to call it to your attention.'

Confucius asks:

'If a train station is where the train stops and a bus station is where the bus stops, what is a work station?'

WHY GOD NEVER RECEIVED TENURE AT UNIVERSITY

1. Because he had only one major publication. And it was in Hebrew. And it had no cited references. And it wasn't published in a journal or even submitted for peer review. And some even doubt he wrote it himself.
2. It may be true that he created the world but what has he done since?
3. The scientific community has had a very rough time trying to replicate his results.
4. He never applied to the Ethics Board for permission to use human subjects.
5. When one experiment went awry, he tried to cover it up by drowning the subjects.
6. He rarely came to class, just told students to read the book.
7. Although there were only ten requirements, most students failed his tests.

A travelling salesman was held up by a tropical storm in the Hawaiian Islands.

He sent an email to his corporate headquarters advising them that he was stranded for a few days and requested instructions.

The reply came back shortly, 'Begin vacation as of yesterday.'

Two women were comparing notes on the difficulties of running a small business.

'I started a new practice last year,' the first one said. 'I insist that each of my employees take at least a week off every three months.'

'Why in the world would you do that?' the other asked.

She responded, 'It's the best way I know of to learn which ones I can do without.'

A fellow stopped at a rural petrol station and, after filling his tank, he bought a drink.

He stood by his car to drink his lemonade and he watched a couple of men working along the roadside.

One man would dig a hole about a metre deep and then move on. The other man came along behind and filled in the hole. While one was digging a new hole, the other was about eight metres behind filling in the old.

'Hold it, hold it,' the fellow said to the men. 'Can you tell me what's going on here with this digging?'

'Well, we work for the council,' one of the men said.

'But one of you is digging a hole and the other is filling it up. You're not accomplishing anything. Aren't you wasting the council's money?'

'You don't understand, mister,' one of the men said, leaning on his shovel and wiping his brow.

'Normally there's three of us, me, Joe and Mike. I dig the hole, Joe sticks in the tree and Mike here puts the dirt back.'

'Yeah,' piped up Mike. 'Now just because Joe is sick, that doesn't mean we can't work, does it?'

Negotiations between union members and their employer were at an impasse. The union denied that their workers were flagrantly abusing sick-leave provisions.

One morning at the bargaining table, the company's chief negotiator held aloft the morning edition of the newspaper, 'This man,' he announced, 'called in sick yesterday!'

There on the sports page, was a photo of the supposedly ill employee, who had just won a local golf tournament with an excellent score.

A union negotiator broke the silence in the room, 'Wow,' he said. 'Think of what kind of score he could have had if he hadn't been sick!'

OFFICE TRUISMS:

Length of lunch breaks is directly proportional to the size of pay packets.

After any salary raise, you will have less money at the end of the month than you did before.

Don't be irreplaceable; if you cannot be replaced, you cannot be promoted.

Hard work never killed anybody. But why take a chance?

Anyone can do any amount of work, provided it isn't the work he is supposed to be doing.

The reward for a job well done is more work.

'I have to have a raise,' the man said to his boss. 'There are three other companies after me.'

'Is that so?' asked the manager. 'What other companies are after you?'

'The electric company, the telephone company and the gas company.'

A big company offered $50 for each money-saving idea submitted by its employees.

First prize went to the employee who suggested the award be cut to $25.

One day a fisherman was lying on a beautiful beach, with his fishing pole propped up in the sand and his solitary line cast out into the sparkling blue surf.

He was enjoying the warmth of the afternoon sun and the prospect of catching a fish.

About that time, a businessman came walking down the beach, trying to relieve some of the stress of his workday.

He noticed the fisherman sitting on the beach and decided to find out why this fisherman was fishing instead of working harder to make a living for himself and his family.

'You aren't going to catch many fish that way,' said the businessman to the fisherman, 'You should be working rather than lying on the beach!'

The fisherman looked up at the businessman, smiled and replied, 'And what will my reward be?'

'Well, you can get bigger nets and catch more fish!' was the businessman's answer.

'And then what will my reward be?' asked the fisherman, still smiling.

The businessman replied, 'You will make money and you'll be able to buy a boat, which will then result in larger catches of fish!'

'And then what will my reward be?' asked the fisherman again.

The businessman was beginning to get a little irritated with the fisherman's questions. 'You can buy a bigger boat and hire some people to work for you!' he said.

'And then what will my reward be?' repeated the fisherman.

The businessman was getting angry. 'Don't you understand? You can build up a fleet of fishing boats, sail all over the world and let all your employees catch fish for you!'

Once again the fisherman asked, 'And then what will my reward be?'

The businessman was red with rage and shouted at the fisherman, 'Don't you understand that you can become so rich that you will never have to work for your living again! You can spend all the rest of your days sitting on this beach, looking at the sunset. You won't have a care in the world!'

The fisherman, still smiling, looked up and said, 'And what do you think I'm doing right now?'

IF YOU HAVE HAD A HARD DAY AT THE OFFICE TRY THIS . . .

1. On your way home from work, stop at the pharmacy, go to the thermometers section and purchase a rectal thermometer made by 'Best Thermo'.
2. When you get home, lock your doors, draw the drapes and disconnect the phone so you will not be disturbed during your therapy.
3. Change to very comfortable clothing and lie down on your bed.
4. Open the package and remove the thermometer. Carefully place it on the bedside table so that it will not become chipped or broken.
5. Take out the material that comes with the thermometer and read it.
6. You will notice that in small print there is a statement, 'Every rectal thermometer made by Best Thermo is personally tested'.
7. Now close your eyes and repeat out loud five times, 'I am so glad I do not work for quality control at the Best Thermo Company.'

SMART AND DUMB

Smart man + smart woman = romance.
Smart man + dumb woman = pregnancy.
Dumb man + smart woman = affair.
Dumb man + dumb woman = marriage.

Smart boss + smart employee = profit.
Smart boss + dumb employee = production.
Dumb boss + smart employee = promotion.
Dumb boss + dumb employee = overtime.

MORE TRUISMS:

Experience is something you don't get until just after you need it.

For every action, there is an equal and opposite criticism.

Keep your boss's boss off your boss's back.

Success always occurs in private and failure in full view.

To steal ideas from one person is plagiarism; to steal from many is research.

If at first you don't succeed, destroy all evidence that you tried.

If you are good, you will be assigned all the work. If you are really good, you will get out of it.

AND A FEW MORE TRUISMS

No one is listening until you make a mistake.

A conclusion is the place where you got tired of thinking.

Following the rules will not get the job done.

He who hesitates is probably right.

People who go to conferences are the ones who shouldn't.

Work is accomplished by those employees who are still striving to reach their level of incompetence.

The only person getting his work done by Friday was Robinson Crusoe.

WHEN I . . .

When I take a long time, I am slow.
When my boss takes a long time, he is thorough.

When I don't do it, I am lazy.
When my boss doesn't do it, he is too busy.

When I do something without being told, I am trying to be smart.

When my boss does the same, that is initiative.

When I succeed, my boss never remembers.

When I fail, he never forgets.

When I make a mistake, I am an idiot.

When my boss makes a mistake, he's only human.

When I am out of the office, I am wandering around.

When my boss is out of the office, he's on business.

DOCTOR, DOCTOR!

A woman takes her 16-year-old daughter to the doctor. The doctor says, 'Okay, Mrs Smith, what's the problem?'

The mother says, 'It's my daughter Lynda. She keeps getting these cravings, she's putting on weight and is sick most mornings.'

The doctor gives Lynda an examination, then turns to the mother and says, 'Well, I don't know how to tell you this, but your Lynda is pregnant—about four months, would be my guess.'

The mother says, 'Pregnant?! She can't be! She has never ever been left alone with a man! Have you, Lynda?'

Lynda says, 'No mother! I've never even kissed a man!'

At this point, the doctor walks over to the window and just stares out. After a few minutes of silence the mother finally asks, 'Is there something wrong doctor?'

The doctor replies, 'No, not really, it's just that the last time anything like this happened, a star appeared in the east and three wise men came over the hill. I'll be darned if I'm going to miss it this time!'

A cardiac specialist died and at his funeral the coffin was placed in front of a huge heart made of flowers.

When the pastor finished with the sermon and after everyone said their tearful good-byes, the big heart of flowers opened, the coffin rolled inside and the heart closed.

Just then one of the mourners burst into laughter.

The guy next to him asked, 'Why are you laughing?'

'I was thinking about my own funeral,' the man replied.

'What's so funny about that?'

'I'm a gynaecologist.'

A woman accompanied her husband to the doctor's office. After his check-up, the doctor called the wife into his office alone.

He said, 'Your husband is suffering from a very severe stress disorder. If you don't follow my instructions carefully, your husband will surely die.

'Each morning, fix him a healthy breakfast. Be pleasant at all times. For lunch make him a nutritious meal. For dinner prepare an especially nice meal for him.

'Don't burden him with chores. Don't discuss your problems with him; it will only make his stress worse. Do not nag him. Most importantly, make love to him regularly. If you can do this for the next ten months to a year, I think your husband will regain his health completely.'

On the way home, the husband asked his wife, 'What did the doctor say?'

'He said you're going to die,' she replied.

'D oc,' says Steve, 'I want to be castrated.'
'What on earth for?' asks the doctor in amazement.

'It's something I've been thinking about for a long time and I want to have it done,' replies Steve.

'But have you thought it through properly?' asks the doctor, 'It's a very serious operation and once it's done, there's no going back. It will change your life forever!'

'I'm aware of that and you're not going to change my mind— either you book me in to be castrated or I'll simply go to another doctor.'

'Well, okay,' says the doctor, 'But it's against my better judgment!'

So Steve has his operation and the next day he is up and walking very slowly, legs apart, down the hospital corridor with his drip stand. Heading towards him is another patient, who is walking exactly the same way.

'Hi there,' says Steve, 'It looks as if you've just had the same operation as me.'

'Well,' said the patient, 'I finally decided after 37 years of life that I would like to be circumcised.'

Steve stared at him in horror and screamed, 'Shit! THAT'S the word!'

A n attractive young girl, chaperoned by an ugly old lady, entered the doctor's office.

'We have come for an examination,' said the young girl.

'All right,' said the doctor, 'Go behind that curtain and take your clothes off.'

'No, not me,' said the girl. 'It's my old aunt here.'

'Very well,' said the doctor. 'Madam, stick out your tongue.'

A man goes to the doctor and tells him that he hasn't been feeling well. The doctor examines him, leaves the room and comes back with three different bottles of pills.

The doctor says, 'Take the green pill with a big glass of water when you get up. Take the blue pill with a big glass of water after lunch. Then just before going to bed, take the red pill with another big glass of water.'

Startled to be put on so much medicine, the man stammers, 'Heavens! What exactly is my problem?'

Doctor says, 'You're not drinking enough water.'

DRINKS ALL ROUND

Two office workers went into a café at lunch-time and ordered two drinks.

They then produced sandwiches from their briefcases and started to eat.

Spying this, the waiter marched over and said to them, 'You can't eat your own sandwiches in here!'

The office workers looked at each other, shrugged their shoulders and then exchanged sandwiches.

A travelling salesman broke down in the Sahara Desert. He decided that his only chance of survival was to find help so he began walking. The sun was relentless and as time passed he became thirsty.

Yet he kept walking.

More time passed and he began feeling faint.

But he kept walking.

Just as he was on the verge of passing out he spied a tent about 500 metres in front of him.

Barely conscious, he reached the tent and called out, 'Water . . .'

A salesman appeared in the tent door and replied sympathetically, 'I am sorry, sir, but I have no water. However, would you like to buy a tie?'

With this, he brandished a collection of exquisite silken neckwear.

'You fool,' gasped the man. 'I'm dying! I need water!'

'Well, sir,' replied the man, 'If you really need water, there is a tent about two kilometres south of here where you can get some.'

ADULTS ONLY OFFICE JOKES

Without knowing how, the man summoned sufficient strength to drag his parched body the distance to the second tent.

With his last ounce of strength he tugged at the door of the tent and collapsed.

Another man, dressed in a costly tuxedo, appeared at the door and asked, 'May I help you sir?'

'Water . . .' was the feeble reply.

'Oh, sir,' came the reply, 'I'm sorry, but you can't come in here without a tie!'

A recently sacked share trader rushes into a bar and orders four expensive 30-year-old single malts.

He lines them up and without pausing quickly downs each one.

'Whew,' the bartender remarked, 'you seem to be in a hurry.'

'You would be too if you had what I have.'

'What do you have?' the bartender sympathetically asked.

'Fifty cents.'

A fter a Beer Festival in London, all the brewery presidents decided to go out for a beer. Corona's president sits down and says, 'Señor, I would like the world's best beer, a Corona.'

The bartender takes a bottle from the shelf and gives it to him.

Then Budweiser's president says, 'I'd like the best beer in the world, give me "The King Of Beers", a Budweiser.'

The bartender gives him one.

Coors' president says, 'I'd like the best beer in the world, the only one made with Rocky Mountain spring water, give me a Coors.'

He gets it.

The guy from Victoria Bitter sits down and says, 'Give me a Coke.'

50 • ADULTS ONLY OFFICE JOKES

The other brewery presidents look over at him amazed and ask, 'Why aren't you drinking a VB?'

The VB boss replies, 'Well, if you guys aren't drinking beer, neither will I.'

THIS ENGINEERING LIFE

Three engineers and three accountants are travelling by train to a conference. At the station the three accountants each buy tickets and watch as the three engineers buy only a single ticket. 'How are three people going to travel on only one ticket?' asks an accountant.

'Watch and you'll see,' answers an engineer.

They all board the train, the accountants taking their seats and the engineers all cramming into the toilet and shutting the door. Shortly after the train has departed, the conductor comes around collecting tickets. He knocks on the toilet door and says, 'Ticket, please.' The door opens just a crack and a single arm emerges with a ticket in hand. The conductor takes it and moves on.

The accountants saw this and agreed it was quite a clever idea. So after the conference, the accountants decide to copy the engineers on the return trip and save some money. When they get to the station they buy a single ticket for the return trip. To their astonishment, the engineers don't buy a ticket at all. 'How are you going to travel without a ticket?' says one perplexed accountant. 'Watch and you'll see,' answers an engineer.

When they board the train the three accountants cram into a restroom and the three engineers cram into another one nearby. The train departs. Shortly afterward, one of the engineers leaves his restroom and walks over to the restroom where the accountants are hiding. He knocks on the door, 'Ticket, please . . .'

Scientists at NASA have developed a gun built specifically to launch dead chickens at the windscreens of airliners, military jets and space shuttles. The idea is to simulate the frequent incidents of collisions with airborne fowl to test the strength of the windshields. British engineers heard about the gun and were eager to test it on the windshields of their new high speed trains.

Arrangements were made and they fired the first chicken. The engineers stood shocked as the chicken hurtled out of the barrel, crashed into the shatterproof shield, smashed it to smithereens, crashed through the control console, snapped the engineer's backrest in two and embedded itself in the back wall of the cabin.

The horrified Britons sent NASA the disastrous results of the experiment, along with the designs of the windscreen and begged the US scientists for suggestions.

NASA's response was just one sentence, 'Thaw the chicken!'

Three engineering students were sitting around talking between classes, when one brought up the question of who designed the human body.

One of the students insisted that the human body must have been designed by an electrical engineer because of the perfection of the nerves and synapses.

Another disagreed and exclaimed that it had to have been a mechanical engineer who designed the human body. The system of levers and pulleys is ingenious.

'No,' the third student said, 'You are both wrong. An architect designed the human body. Who else but an architect would put a toxic waste line through a recreation area . . .?'

An engineer, an accountant, a chemist and a bureaucrat were bragging about how smart their dogs are.

To settle who had the smartest dog they agreed to put their dogs through their paces.

The engineer called to his dog, 'T-square, do your stuff.'

The dog took out paper and pen, drew a circle, a square and a triangle. Everyone was suitably impressed.

The accountant called, 'Taxation, do your stuff.'

The pooch went to the kitchen, got a dozen cookies and made four stacks of three. The others nodded their surprise.

So the chemist called, 'Beaker, do your stuff.'

The dog went to the fridge for a bottle of milk, got a 300 mm glass and poured exactly 275 mm without spilling a drop. Everyone agreed that was great.

Finally it was the bureaucrat's turn. 'Coffee-Break, do your stuff!' he roared.

Coffee-Break ate the cookies, drank the milk, chewed the paper, claimed he injured his mouth doing so, filed a grievance for unsafe working conditions, put in for workers' compensation and took extended sick leave.

REAL ENGINEERS

- Real Engineers consider themselves well dressed if their socks match.
- Real engineers have a non-technical vocabulary of 800 words.
- Real Engineers say, 'It's 70 degrees Fahrenheit, 25 degrees Celsius and 298 Kelvin,' and all you say is, 'Isn't it a nice day?'
- Real Engineers wear badges so they don't forget who they are.

Sometimes a note is attached saying 'Don't offer me a lift today. I drove my own car'.

- Real Engineers know how to take the cover off their computer and are not afraid to do it.
- Real Engineers don't find the above at all funny.

THE DICTIONARY: WHAT ENGINEERS SAY AND WHAT THEY MEAN

Major Technological Breakthrough.
(Back to the drawing board.)

Developed after years of intensive research.
(Discovered by accident.)

Test results were extremely gratifying.
(It works and are we surprised!)

Customer satisfaction is believed assured.
(We are so far behind schedule that the customer was happy to get anything at all.)

Project slightly behind original schedule due to unforeseen difficulties.
(We are working on something else.)

A number of different approaches are being tried.
(We don't know where we're going.)

Extensive effort is being applied on a fresh approach to the problem.
(We just hired three new guys; they might have an idea.)

Preliminary operational tests are inconclusive.
(The thing blew up when we threw the switch.)

The entire concept will have to be abandoned.
(The only guy who understood the thing quit.)

Essentially complete.
(Half done.)

We predict . . .
(We hope . . .)

Serious, but not insurmountable, problems.
(It will take a miracle.)

Requires further analysis and management attention.
(Totally out of control.)

The software is being developed without excessive process overhead.
(The documentation will be written in clear and lucid Chinese.)

FOR ART'S SAKE

An artist asked the gallery owner if there had been any interest in his paintings on display at that time.

'I have good news and bad news,' the owner replied. 'The good news is that a gentleman inquired about your work and wondered if it would appreciate in value after your death. When I told him it would, he bought all 15 of your paintings.'

'That's wonderful,' the artist exclaimed. 'What's the bad news?'

'The guy was your doctor . . .'

A world famous painter, in the prime of her career, started losing her eyesight. Fearful that she might lose her livelihood as a painter, she went to see the best eye surgeon in the world.

After several weeks of delicate surgery and therapy, her eyesight was restored. The painter was so grateful that she decided to show her gratitude by repainting the doctor's office.

Part of her work included painting a gigantic eye on one wall. When she had finished her work, she held a press conference to unveil her latest work of art at the doctor's office.

During the press conference, one reporter noticed the eye on the wall and asked the doctor, 'What was your first reaction upon seeing your newly painted office, especially that large eye on the wall?'

To this, the eye doctor responded, 'I said to myself 'Thank God I'm not a proctologist.'

An artist had been working on a nude portrait for a long time. Every day, he was up early and worked late—bringing perfection with every stroke of his paint-brush. As each day passed, he gained a better understanding of the female body and was able to really make his paintings shine.

After a month, the artist had become very weary from this non-stop effort and decided to take it easy for the day. Since his model had already shown up, he suggested they merely have a glass of wine and talk—since normally he preferred to do his painting in silence.

They talked for a few hours, getting to know each other better.

Then as they were sipping their claret, the artist heard a car arriving outside. He jumped up and said, 'Oh no! It's my wife! Quick, take off your clothes!'

GETTING THAT JOB

NEW JOB INTERVIEW TECHNIQUE

Take the prospective employee and put him in a room with only a table and two chairs. Leave him alone for two hours, without any instruction. At the end of that time, go back and see what he is doing.

- If he has taken the table apart, put him in Engineering.
- If he is counting the butts in the ashtray, assign him to Accounting.
- If he is waving his arms and talking out loud, send him to Consulting.
- If he is talking to the chairs, Personnel is a good spot for him.
- If he is sleeping, he is Management material.
- If he doesn't even look up when you enter the room, assign him to Security.
- If he tries to tell you it's not as bad as it looks, put him into Marketing.
- If he mentions what a good price he got for the table and chairs, send him to Sales.
- If he mentions that hardwood furniture does not come from rainforests, Public Relations will suit him well.

'Why are you so excited?', the surgeon asked the patient that was about to be anaesthetised.

'But Doc, this is my first operation.'

'Really? It's mine too and I am not excited at all.'

A young man, hired by a supermarket, reported for his first day of work.

The manager greeted him with a warm handshake and a smile, gave him a broom and said, 'Your first job will be to sweep out the store.'

'But I'm a college graduate,' the young man replied indignantly.

'Oh, I'm sorry. I didn't know that,' said the manager. 'Here, give me the broom, I'll show you how.'

A manager of a retail clothing store is reviewing a potential employee's application and notices that the man has never worked in retail before.

He says to the man, 'For a man with no experience, you are certainly asking for a high wage.'

'Well Sir,' the applicant replies, 'the work is so much harder when you don't know what you're doing!'

The classified ad read, 'Wanted: a very experienced lumberjack'. A man answered the ad and was asked to describe his experience.

'Well,' he said 'I've worked at the Sahara Forest.'

'You mean the Sahara Desert,' said the interviewer.

The man laughed and answered, 'Oh sure, that's what they call it now!'

EXPERIENCE IS . . .

- Experience is directly proportional to the amount of equipment ruined.
- Experience is something you do not get until just after you need it.
- Experience is what causes a person to make new mistakes instead of old ones.
- Experience is what you get when you were expecting something else.

- Experience is knowledge acquired when it's too late.
- Experience is that marvellous thing that enables you to recognise a mistake when you make it again.

THE ELEPHANT HUNT

- Mathematicians hunt elephants by going to Africa, throwing out everything that is not an elephant and catching one of whatever is left.
- Experienced mathematicians will prove the existence of at least one unique elephant and then leave the detection and capture of an actual elephant as an exercise for their graduate students.
- Economists don't hunt elephants, but they believe that if elephants are paid enough, they will hunt themselves.
- Experienced economists never saw an elephant, but they try to hunt one by controlling the interest rates.
- Statisticians hunt the first grey animal they see N times and call it an elephant.
- Experienced statisticians add that there is a small probability that the animal they hunted is a mouse.
- Lawyers can let hunting a single elephant drag out for several years.
- Experienced lawyers can make it last even longer.
- Consultants don't hunt elephants and many have never hunted anything at all, but they can be hired by the hour to advise those people who do.
- Experienced consultants can also measure the correlation of hat size and bullet colour to the efficiency of elephant-hunting strategies, if someone else will only identify the elephants.
- Politicians don't hunt elephants, but they will share the elephants you catch with the people who voted for them.
- Experienced politicians take the elephant for themselves and blame the press.

- Managers set broad elephant-hunting policy based on the assumption that elephants are just like field mice, but with deeper voices.
- Experienced managers keep in the project file the advice that claims that elephants are just like field mice.
- Sales people don't hunt elephants but spend their time selling elephants they haven't caught, for delivery two days before the season opens.
- Experienced sales people ship the first thing they catch and write up an invoice for an elephant.
- Computer sales people catch grey animals at random and sell them.
- Experienced computer sales people catch grey rabbits and sell them as desktop elephants.

S ome tourists in the Melbourne Museum are marvelling at the dinosaur bones. One of them asks the guard, 'Can you tell me how old the dinosaur bones are?'

The guard replies, 'They are three million, four years and six months old.'

'That's an awfully exact number,' says the tourist. 'How do you know their age so precisely?'

The guard answers, 'Well, the dinosaur bones were three million years old when I started working here and that was four and a half years ago.'

H arry gets a new job at the zoo. On his first morning he is given three tasks.

The first is to weed the exotic fish pool. Harry wades in and starts to weed, when suddenly a bloody great fish leaps out and bites him. Enraged, Harry beats the offending fish to death.

Upon doing so he realises that his boss is not going to be pleased, so Harry tries to hide the dead fish. In a flash of inspiration he decided to feed the fish to the lions—as lions will eat anything. So Harry feeds the fish to the lions.

Harry's second job is to clear out the monkey house. Harry is shovelling away when a couple of chimps start throwing shit at him. Harry has a short temper and finds himself beating the chimps with his spade. The chimps are killed instantly.

Harry realises he needs to dispose of the bodies. So he decides to feed the chimps to the lions—because lions eat anything.

Harry's last job is to collect honey from some South American bees. Harry begins to clean the hives out when suddenly the bees start swarming and stinging him repeatedly. Harry loses it and swipes the whole swarm of bees to death.

He is unfazed at the carnage because he knows what to do. That's right, he feeds them to the lions—because lions eat anything.

Later that day a new lion arrives at the zoo. It wanders up to another lion and says 'What's the food like here?'

The other lion says, 'Absolutely brilliant, today I had fish and chimps with mushy bees.'

A tourist walks into a pet shop in Silicon Valley and is browsing round the cages on display.

While he is there another customer walks in and says to the shopkeeper, 'I'll have a C monkey, please.'

The shopkeeper nods, goes over to a cage at the side of the shop and takes out a monkey. He fits a collar and leash and hands it to the customer, saying 'That'll be $5000.'

The customer pays and walks out with his monkey.

Startled, the tourist goes over to the shopkeeper. 'That was a very expensive monkey—most of them are only a few hundred dollars. Why did it cost so much?'

'Ah, that monkey can program in C—very fast, tight code, no bugs, well worth the money.'

The tourist takes another look at the monkeys in the cage.

He sees one that is even more expensive, selling for $10,000 dollars! 'What does that one do?' he asks.

'Oh, that one's a C++ monkey; it can manage object oriented programming, Visual C++, even Windows, all the really useful stuff,' replied the salesman.

The tourist looks round for a little longer and sees a third monkey in a cage on its own. The price tag round its neck says $50,000.

He gasps to the shopkeeper, 'That one costs more than all the others put together! What on earth does it do?'

'Well, I don't know if it does anything, but it says it's a Contractor.'

GOODBYE AND FAREWELL...

Luke is called into the boss's office. After several minutes Luke emerges from the office, slams the door and shakes his fist at the door.

'I'm never going to work for that man again!' he rages.

'Why, what did he say?' asked his colleagues.

'You're fired!'

A boss calls into his office four of his employees and says, 'I'm really sorry, but the company has fallen on hard times and unfortunately I'm going to have to let one of you go.'

Sam, who is an African American, speaks first, 'Well I would just like to point out that under equal opportunity laws I'm a protected minority.'

Barbara chips in, 'And I'm a woman working in a male dominated sector.'

Stan, who is nearing retirement age, says 'Fire me, buster and I'll hit you with an age discrimination suit so fast it'll make your head spin.'

They all turn to Gary, a young, white, male employee. There is a moment's silence until he says, 'I think I might be gay . . .'

The four word story of employment:
Hired.
Tired.
Mired.
Fired.

HARD AND SOFT ... WARE

COMPUTER DEFINITIONS

- Bit—a word used to describe computers, as in 'our daughter's computer cost quite a bit'.
- Boot—what your friends give you because you spend too much time bragging about your computer skills.
- Bug—what your eyes do after you stare at the tiny green computer screen for more than 15 minutes.
- Chips—the fattening, non-nutritional food computer users eat to avoid having to leave their keyboards.
- Cursor—what you turn into when you can't get your computer to perform, as in 'you damn computer!'
- Disk—what goes out of your back after bending over a computer keyboard for seven hours at a time.
- Dump—the place all your former hobbies wind up soon after you install games on your computer.
- Error—what you made when you first walked into a computer showroom 'just to look'.
- Expansion unit—the new room you have to build on to your home to house your computer and all its peripherals.
- File—what a secretary can now do to her nails six and a half hours a day, now that the computer does her day's work in 30 minutes.
- Floppy—the condition of a constant computer user's stomach due to lack of exercise and a steady diet of junk food (see 'Chips').

- Hardware—tools, such as lawnmowers, rakes and other heavy equipment you haven't laid a finger on since getting your computer.
- IBM—the kind of missile your family members and friends would like to drop on your computer so you'll pay attention to them again.
- Menu—what you'll never see again after buying a computer because you'll be too poor to eat in a restaurant.
- Programs—those things you used to look at on your television before you hooked your computer up.
- Return—what lots of people do to their computers after they receive their first billing from their internet service provider.
- Terminal—a place where you can find buses, trains and really good deals on hot computers.
- Windows—what you heave the computer out of after you accidentally erase a program that took you three days to set up.

An email from a blonde Y2K engineer

To: Manager

I have completed the task as requested, but to be honest, none of this Y to K problem makes any sense to me.

At any rate, I have finished converting all the months on all the company calendars so that the year 2000 is ready to go with the following new months:

Januark Februark Mak Julk.

Regards,
Rob

WRONG ADDRESS

Mr Steve Johnson, a businessman from Wisconsin, went on a business trip to Louisiana.

When he arrived, he immediately sent an email back home to his wife, Jennifer. Unfortunately, he mistyped a letter in the address and the email ended up going to a Mrs Joan Johnson, the wife of a preacher who had just passed away.

The preacher's wife took one look at the email and promptly fainted.

When she was finally revived, she nervously pointed to the message, which read, 'Arrived safely, but it sure is hot down here.'

While my brother-in-law was tapping away on his home computer, his ten-year-old daughter sneaked up behind him. Then she turned and ran into the kitchen, squealing to the rest of the family, 'I know Daddy's password! I know Daddy's password!'

'What is it?' her sisters asked eagerly.

Proudly she replied, 'Asterisk, asterisk, asterisk, asterisk, asterisk!'

A helicopter was flying around above Seattle, when an electrical malfunction disabled all of the aircraft's electronic navigation and communications equipment.

Due to the clouds and haze, the pilot could not determine the helicopter's position nor the course to steer to the airport.

The pilot saw a tall building, flew towards it and circled it. He wrote a sign and held it in the helicopter's window. The pilot's sign said 'WHERE AM I?' in large letters.

People in the tall building quickly responded to the aircraft, drew a large sign and held it in a building window. Their sign said 'YOU ARE IN A HELICOPTER'.

The pilot smiled, waved, looked at his map, determined the course to steer to Seattle airport and landed safely.

After they were on the ground, the co-pilot asked the pilot how the 'YOU ARE IN A HELICOPTER' sign helped determine their position in Seattle.

The pilot responded 'I knew that had to be the Microsoft building because, similar to their help lines, they gave me a technically correct but completely useless answer.'

J esus and Satan are having a furious argument as to who is the better computer programmer.

They decide to hold a competition and ask God to be the judge. They set themselves up on their computers and begin. They type furiously, lines of code steaming up the screen, for several hours straight.

Seconds before the end of the competition, a bolt of lightning strikes, taking out the electricity. Moments later, the power is restored and God announces the contest is over.

God asks Satan to show what he has come up with. Satan is visibly upset and cries, 'I have nothing. I lost it all when the power went out.'

'Very well, then,' says God, 'Let us see if Jesus fared any better.'

Jesus enters a command and the screen comes to life in a vivid display, the voices of an angelic choir pouring forth from the speakers.

Satan is astonished. He stutters, 'But how?! I lost everything, yet Jesus' program is intact? How did he do it?'

God chuckles, 'Everybody knows . . . Jesus saves.'

B ill Gates (CEO of Microsoft), Andy Grove (CEO of Intel) and Jerry Sanders (CEO of AMD) were in a high-powered business meeting. During the serious, tense discussions, a beeping noise suddenly is emitted from where Bill is sitting.

Bill says, 'Oh, that's my emergency beeper. Gentlemen, excuse me, I really need to take this call.'

So Bill lifts his wristwatch to his ear and begins talking into the end of his tie. After completing this call, he notices the others are staring at him.

Bill explains, 'Oh, this is my new emergency communication system. I have an earpiece built into my watch and a microphone sewn into the end of my tie. That way, I can a take a call anywhere.'

The others nod and the meeting continues.

Five minutes later, the discussion is again interrupted when Andy starts beeping. He also states, 'Oh, that is my emergency beeper. Excuse me, gentlemen, this must be an important call.'

So Andy taps his earlobe and begins talking into thin air.

When he completes his call, he notices the others staring at him and explains, 'I also have an emergency communication system. But my earpiece is actually implanted in my earlobe and the microphone is actually embedded in this fake tooth. Isn't that neat?'

The others nod and the meeting continues.

Five minutes later, the discussion is again interrupted when Jerry emits a thunderous fart.

He looks up at the others staring at him and says, 'Uh, somebody get me a piece of paper . . . I'm receiving a fax.'

Bill Gates meets Hugh Grant at a Hollywood party.
They are talking and Bill says, 'I've seen some great pictures of Divine Brown lately, I sure would like to get together with her!'

Hugh replies, 'Well Bill, you know . . . ever since our incident, her price has skyrocketed. She's charging a small fortune.'

Bill said with a chuckle, 'Hugh, money's no object to me. What's her number?'

So, Hugh gives Bill her number and Bill sets up a date.

They meet and after they finish, Bill is lying there in ecstasy, mumbling, 'God . . . now I know why you chose the name Divine.'

To which she replies, 'Thank you Bill . . . And now I know how you chose the name Microsoft.'

There are three engineers in a car—an electrical engineer, a chemical engineer and a Microsoft engineer.

Suddenly the car loses power and rolls to a stop by the side of the road. The three engineers look at each other wondering what could be wrong.

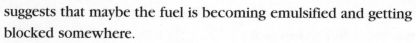

The electrical engineer suggests stripping down the electronics of the car and trying to trace where a fault might have occurred.

The chemical engineer, not knowing much about cars, suggests that maybe the fuel is becoming emulsified and getting blocked somewhere.

Then the Microsoft engineer, not knowing much about anything, says, 'Why don't we close all the windows, get out, get back in, open the windows again and maybe it will work?'

IN THE GOOD OLD DAYS . . .

- An application was for employment.
- A program was a TV show.
- A keyboard was a piano.
- Memory was something that you lost with age.
- If you unzipped anything in public, you'd be jailed.
- Log on was adding wood to a fire.
- Hard drive was a long trip on the road.
- A mouse pad was where a mouse lived.
- A backup happened to your commode.
- Cut, you did with a pocket knife.

- Paste, you did with glue.
- A web was a spider's home.
- A virus was the flu.
- And if you had a 3 1/2 inch floppy, you hoped nobody found out!

MEMO

New Software

This memo is to announce the development of a new software system that is Year 2000 compliant.

The program is known as 'Millennium Year Application Software System' (MYASS).

Next Monday there will be a meeting in which I will show MYASS to everyone.

We will hold demonstrations throughout the month so that all employees will have an opportunity to get a good look at MYASS. We have not addressed networking aspects yet, so currently only one person at a time can use MYASS. This restriction will be removed after MYASS expands.

Some employees have begun using the program already. This morning I walked into a subordinate's office and was not surprised to find that he had his nose buried in MYASS.

Some of the less technical people may be somewhat afraid of MYASS. Last week my Personal Assistant said to me, 'I'm a little nervous, I never put anything in MYASS before.' I helped her and afterward she admitted that it was relatively painless and she was actually looking forward to doing it again and was even ready to kiss MYASS.

There have been concerns over the virus that was found in MYASS upon initial installation, but the virus has been eliminated and we were able to save MYASS. In the future, however, protection will be required prior to entering MYASS.

This database will encompass all information associated with the business. As you begin using the program, feel free to put anything you want in MYASS.

As MYASS grows larger, we envision a time when it will be commonplace for a supervisor to hand work to an employee and say, 'Here, stick this in MYASS.'

It will be a great day when we need data quickly and our employees can respond, 'Here it is, I just pulled it out of MYASS.'

AN INTERNET PROVIDER'S ONLINE MESSAGES FOR UNLIMITED HOURS CUSTOMERS

You have been on-line for 46 minutes. Do you want to stay on-line? Please respond within 10 minutes or you will be logged off.

You have been on-line 135 minutes. Not to put any pressure on you, but there are other people in the world who would like to sign on. Let's show some consideration for our fellow members and sign off. What do you say?

You do realise that you have been on-line for 180 minutes, right? When was the last time you went outside?

Okay, this is getting ridiculous. Frankly, you're starting to upset us! If you sign off now, we'll bring back your buddy list, okay?

You have been on-line for 360 minutes now! We promised you unlimited time, we know, but can't you just finish up and go read a good book?

You have been on-line for 467 minutes. Surely you have a job to go to?

You have been on-line for 513 minutes. Your spouse has left and your dog is starving. Do you wish to remain on-line?

You have been on-line for 724 minutes. Maybe someone might actually be trying to get through on the phone line? But then again you probably don't have friends.

You have been on-line for 852 minutes. Do you know how many hours that is?

You have been on-line for 967 minutes. When your provider went to unlimited hours they didn't think you would take it literally! So get off before we go broke!

You have been on-line for 1105 minutes. Have you opened a 24 hour internet café right there in your lounge room? GET OFF!

You have been on-line 1251 minutes. Welcome to the team, computer-geek! See job application enclosed.

At a recent computer expo, Bill Gates compared the computer industry to the automotive industry by saying 'If General Motors had kept up with technology like the computer industry has, we would all be driving cars that cost $25.00 and get 1000 miles to the gallon.'

In response to Bill's comment, General Motors issued a press release making the following statement:

'If General Motors had kept up with technology like the computer industry has, we would all be driving cars with the following characteristics:

1. For no reason whatsoever your car would crash twice per day.
2. Every time they repainted the lines in the road, you would have to buy a new car.

3. Your car would occasionally stop on the freeway without reason. In order to get it started again, you would have to push it to the side of the road, close all the windows, turn off the car, restart the car and open all the windows again. You would simply do this without question.

4. Occasionally your car would inexplicably shut down and refuse to restart. In this instance you would have to reinstall the engine.

5. You would press the 'start' button to shut off the engine.

6. The oil warning light, water warning light, fuel light and alternator warning light would all be replaced by a single 'Unidentified System Error' light.

7. The air bag would ask your mangled body, 'Are you sure?' before going off.

8. Sporadically, for no reason whatsoever, your car would lock you out and refuse to let you back in until you simultaneously lifted the driver side door handle, turned the key and grabbed the radio antenna.

9. The radio antenna would be internally mounted on the passenger side of the car.

10. Macintosh would make a car that was five times faster, ten times more reliable and easier to maintain, twice as easy to drive, but would only run on five percent of the roads.'

A software engineer, hardware engineer and departmental manager were on their way to a meeting in Switzerland.

They were driving down a steep mountain road when suddenly the brakes failed. The car careened out of control, bouncing off guardrails, until it miraculously ground to a scraping halt along the mountainside.

The occupants of the car were unhurt, but they had a problem. They were stuck halfway down the mountain in a car with no brakes.

'I know,' said the manager. 'Let's have a meeting, propose a vision, formulate a mission statement, define some goals and through a process of continuous improvement, find a solution to the critical problems and we'll be on our way.'

'No,' said the hardware engineer. 'I've got my Swiss army knife with me. I can strip down the car's braking system, isolate the fault, fix it and we'll be on our way.'

'Wait,' said the software engineer. 'Before we do anything, shouldn't we push the car back to the top of the mountain and see if it happens again?'

ACTUAL DIALOGUE OF A FORMER COMPUTER SUPPORT EMPLOYEE

'**C**ustomer Support; may I help you?'
'Yes, well, I'm having trouble with my computer.'
'What sort of trouble?'
'Well, I was just typing along and all of a sudden the words went away.'
'Went away?'
'They disappeared.'
'Hmm. So what does your screen look like now?'
'Nothing.'
'Nothing?'
'It's blank; it won't accept anything when I type.'
'Are you still in Word or did you get out?'
'How do I tell?'
'Can you see the C: prompt on the screen?'
'What's a sea-prompt?'
'Never mind. Can you move the cursor around on the screen?'
'There isn't any cursor: I told you, it won't accept anything I type.'
'Does your monitor have a power indicator?'
'What's a monitor?'
'It's the thing with the screen on it that looks like a TV. Does it have a little light that tells you when it's on?'

'I don't know.'

'Well, then look on the back of the monitor and find where the power cord goes into it. Can you see that?'

'Yes, I think so.'

'Great! Follow the cord to the plug and tell me if it's plugged into the wall.'

'Yes, it is.'

'When you were behind the monitor, did you notice that there were two cables plugged into the back of it, not just one?'

'No.'

'Well, I need you to look back there again and find the other cable.'

'Okay, here it is.'

'Follow it for me and tell me if it's plugged securely into the back of your computer.'

'I can't reach.'

'Uh huh. Well, can you see if it is?'

'No.'

'Even if you maybe put your knee on something and lean way over?'

'Oh, it's not because I don't have the right angle, it's because it's dark.'

'Dark?'

'Yes the office light is off and the only light I have is coming in from the window.'

'Well, turn on the office light then.'

'I can't.'

'No? Why not?'

'Because there's a power outage.'

'A power . . . A power outage? Aha! Okay, we've got it licked now. Do you still have the boxes and manuals and packing stuff your computer came in?'

'Well, yes, I keep them in the closet.'

'Good! Go get them and unplug your system and pack it up just like it was when you got it. Then take it back to the store you bought it from.'

'Really? Is it that bad?'

'Yes, I'm afraid it is.'

'Well, all right then, I suppose. What do I tell them?'

'Tell them you're too stupid to own a computer.'

HELP ME! HELP ME!

Caller:	Hello, is this the Help Line?
Help Line:	Yes, it is. How may I help you?
Caller:	The cup holder on my PC is broken and I am within my warranty period. How do I go about getting that fixed?
Help Line:	I'm sorry, but did you say a cup holder?
Caller:	Yes, it's attached to the front of my computer.
Help Line:	Please excuse me if I seem a bit stumped, it's because I am. Did you receive this as part of a promotion at a trade show? How did you get this cup holder? Does it have any trademark on it?
Caller:	It came with my computer, I don't know anything about a promotional. It just has '4X' on it.
Help Line:	So this cup holder would actually be your CD-ROM drive. Lady you do not deserve to own a computer!

IMAGINE IF GENERAL MOTORS HAD A HELPLINE FOR THEIR CARS!

Help Line: General Motors Help Line, how can I help you?

Customer: I got in my car and closed the door and nothing happened!

Help Line: Did you put the key in the ignition slot and turn it?

Customer: What's an ignition?

Help Line: It's a starter motor that draws current from your battery and turns over the engine.

Customer: Ignition? Motor? Battery? Engine? How come I have to know all these technical terms just to use my car?

**

Help Line: General Motors Help Line, how can I help you?

Customer: My car ran fine for a week and now it won't go anywhere!

Help Line: Is the petrol tank empty?

Customer: Huh? How do I know?

Help Line: There's a little gauge on the front panel with a needle and markings from 'E' to 'F'. Where is the needle pointing?

Customer: It's pointing to 'E'. What does that mean?

Help Line: It means you have to visit a petrol vendor and purchase some more petrol. You can install it yourself or pay the vendor to install it for you.

Customer: What? I paid $12,000 for this car! Now you tell me that I have to keep buying more components? I want a car that comes with everything built in!

**

Help Line: General Motors Help Line, how can I help you?

Customer: Your cars suck!

Help Line: What's wrong?

Customer: It crashed, that's what's wrong!

Help Line: What were you doing?

Customer: I wanted to run faster, so I pushed the accelerator pedal all the way to the floor. It worked for a while and then it crashed and it won't start now!

Help Line: It's your responsibility if you misuse the product. What do you expect us to do about it?

Customer: I want you to send me one of the latest versions that doesn't crash any more!

**

Help Line: General Motors Help Line, how can I help you?

Customer: Hi, I just bought my first car and I chose your car because it has automatic transmission, cruise control, power steering, power brakes and power door locks.

Help Line: Thanks for buying our car. How can I help you?

Customer: How do I work it?

Help Line: Do you know how to drive?

Customer: Do I know how to what?

Help Line: Do you know how to drive?

Customer: I'm not a technical person. I just want to go places in my car!

HIGHER EDUCATION

A mother and father were worried about their son not wanting to learn mathematics at the school he was in, so they decided to send him to a Catholic school.

After the first day of school, their son came racing into the house, went straight into his room and slammed the door shut.

They were a little worried that he had had a bad day, but when they went to check on him, they found him sitting at his desk doing his homework.

Surprisingly the boy kept this up for the whole year and in his final report received an A+ for mathematics.

The mother and father were ecstatic and asked the son, 'What changed your mind about learning maths?'

The son looked at his mum and dad and said, 'Well, on the first day when I walked into the classroom, I saw a guy nailed to the plus sign at the back of the room behind the teacher's desk and I knew they meant business.'

The science teacher lecturing his class in biology said, 'Now I'll show you this frog in my pocket.'

He then reached into his pocket and pulled out a chicken sandwich.

He looked puzzled for a second, thought deeply and said, 'That's funny. I distinctly remember eating my lunch.'

Isn't the principal a dummy!' said a boy to a girl.

'Say, do you know who I am?' asked the girl.

'No.'

'I'm the principal's daughter.'

'And do you know who I am?' asked the boy.

'No,' she replied.

'Thank goodness!'

THE EVOLUTION OF A MATHS PROBLEM

1950

A lumberjack sells a truckload of lumber for $100. His cost of production is 4/5 of this price. What is his profit?

1960 (traditional math)

A lumberjack sells a truckload of lumber for $100. His cost of production is 4/5 of this price or in other words $80. What is his profit?

1970 (new math)

A lumberjack exchanges a set L of lumber for a set M of money. The cardinality of set M is 100 and each element is worth $1. Make 100 dots representing the elements of set M. The set C is a subset of set M, of cardinality 80. What is the cardinality of the set P of profits, if P is the difference set M\C?

1980 (equal opportunity math)

A lumberjack sells a truckload of wood for $100. His or her cost of production is $80 and his or her profit is $20. Your assignment: Underline the number 20.

1990 (outcome based education)

By cutting down beautiful forest trees, a lumberperson makes $20. What do you think of his way of making a living? In your group, discuss how the forest birds and squirrels feel and write an essay about it.

1995 (entrepreneurial math)

By laying off 402 of its lumberjacks, a company improves its stock price from $80 to $100. How much capital gain per share does the CEO make by exercising his stock options at $80? Assume capital gains are no longer taxed, because this encourages investment.

1998 (motivational math)

A logging company exports its wood-finishing jobs to its Indonesian subsidiary and lays off the corresponding half of its US workers (the higher-paid half). It clear-cuts 95 per cent of the forest, leaving the rest for the spotted owl and lays off all its remaining US workers. It tells the workers that the spotted owl is responsible for the absence of fellable trees and lobbies Congress for exemption from the Endangered Species Act. Congress instead exempts the company from all federal regulation. What is the return on investment of the lobbying?

THE WAY TO GRADE FINAL EXAMS

Department of Statistics
All grades are plotted along the normal bell curve.

Department of Psychology
Students are asked to blot ink in their exam books, close them and turn them in. The professor opens the books and assigns the first grade that comes to mind.

Department of History
All students get the same grade they got last year.

Department of Religion
Grade is determined by God.

Department of Philosophy
What is a grade?

Law School
Students are asked to defend their position of why they should receive an A.

Department of Computer Science
Random number generator determines grade.

Music Department
Each student must figure out his grade by listening to the instructor play the corresponding note.

Department of Physical Education
Everybody gets an A.

An English professor complained to the pet shop proprietor, 'The parrot I purchased uses improper language.'

'I'm surprised,' said the owner. 'I've never taught that bird to swear.'

'Oh, it isn't that,' explained the professor. 'But yesterday I heard him split an infinitive.'

A linguistics professor was lecturing his class the other day. 'In English,' he said, 'A double negative forms a positive. However, in some languages, such as Russian, a double negative remains a negative. But there isn't a single language, not one, in which a double positive can express a negative.'

A voice from the back of the room retorted, 'Yeah, right . . .'

HOW CAREERS END . . .

Lawyers are disbarred.

Ministers are defrocked.

Electricians are delighted.

Far Eastern diplomats are disoriented.

Drunks are distilled.

Orchestra leaders are disbanded.

Artists' models are deposed.

Cooks are deranged.

Office clerks are defiled.

Mediums are dispirited.

Programmers are decoded.

Accountants are discredited.

Holy people are disgraced.

Pastry chefs are deserted.

Perfume makers are dissented.

Butterfly collectors are debugged.

Students are degraded.

Underwear models are debriefed.

Painters are discoloured.

Spinsters are dismissed.

Judges are disappointed.

Casino dealers are discarded.

Mathematicians are discounted.

Tree surgeons disembark.

EXCERPTS FROM ACTUAL LETTERS SENT TO LANDLORDS...

I request your permission to remove my drawers in the kitchen.

The toilet is blocked and we cannot bathe the children until it is cleared.

I want some repairs done to my stove, as it has backfires and burnt my knob off.

The toilet seat is cracked: where do I stand?

I am writing on behalf of my sink, which is running away from the wall.

Our lavatory seat is broken in half and is now in three pieces.

The person next door has a large erection in his back garden, which is unsightly and dangerous.

Will you please send a man to look at my water? It is a funny colour and not fit to drink.

I want to complain about the farmer across the road. Every morning at 5.30 his cock wakes me up and it is getting too much.

CHANGED HR POLICIES

Casual Fridays

Week 1, Memo No. 1
Effective this week, the company is adopting Fridays as Casual Day. Employees are free to dress in the casual attire of their choice.

Week 3, Memo No. 2
Spandex and leather micro-miniskirts are not appropriate attire for Casual Day. Neither are string ties, rodeo belt buckles or moccasins.

Week 6, Memo No. 3
Casual Day refers to dress only, not attitude. When planning Friday's wardrobe, remember image is a key to our success.

Week 8, Memo No. 4
A seminar on how to dress for Casual Day will be held at 4 pm Friday in the cafeteria. A fashion show will follow. Attendance is mandatory.

Week 9, Memo No. 5
As an outgrowth of Friday's seminar, a 14 member Casual Day

Task Force has been appointed to prepare guidelines for proper Casual Day dress.

Week 14, Memo No. 6
The Casual Day Task Force has now completed a 30 page manual entitled 'Relaxing Dress Without Relaxing Company Standards'. A copy has been distributed to every employee. Please review the chapter 'You Are What You Wear' and consult the 'Home Casual' versus 'Business Casual' checklist before leaving for work each Friday. If you have doubts about the appropriateness of an item of clothing, contact your CDTF representative before 7 am on Friday.

Week 18, Memo No. 7
Our Employee Assistant Plan (EAP) has now been expanded to provide support for psychological counselling for employees who may be having difficulty adjusting to Casual Day.

Week 20, Memo No. 8
Due to budget cuts in the HR Department, we are no longer able to effectively support or manage Casual Day. Casual Day will be discontinued, effective immediately.

Reaching the end of a job interview, the Human Resources Person asked the young graduate fresh out of Sydney University, 'And what starting salary were you looking for?'

The candidate said, 'In the neighbourhood of $125,000 a year, depending on the benefits package.'

The HR Person said, 'Well, what would you say to a package of six weeks holiday, 14 rostered days off, full medical and dental, company matching superannuation fund to 50 per cent of salary and a company car leased every two years—say, a red Corvette?'

The Engineer sat up straight and said, 'Wow! Are you kidding?'

And the HR Person said, 'Certainly, but you started it.'

An old blacksmith realised he was soon going to have to retire. He picked out a strong young man to become his apprentice.

The old fellow was crabby and exacting. Curt and blunt in his directions.

'Don't ask me a lot of questions,' he told the boy. 'Just do whatever I tell you to do.'

One day the old blacksmith took an iron out of the forge and laid it on the anvil.

'Get the hammer over there,' he said. 'When I nod my head, hit it real good and hard.'

Now, the blacksmith doesn't have to worry about retirement.

For 30 years, Johnson had arrived at work at 9 am on the dot. He had never taken a sick day and was never late.

Consequently, when on one particular day 9.05 am passed without Johnson's arrival, it caused a sensation. All work ceased and the boss himself, looking at his watch and muttering, came out into the corridor.

Finally, precisely at ten, Johnson showed up. His clothes were dusty and torn. His face was scratched and bruised and his glasses were bent.

He limped painfully to the time clock, punched in. Aware that all eyes were upon him he said, 'I tripped and rolled down two flights of stairs in the subway. Nearly killed myself.'

And the boss said, 'And to roll down two flights of stairs took you a whole hour?'

TEN THINGS YOU'LL NEVER HEAR AN EMPLOYEE TELL THEIR BOSS

1. Never give me work in the morning. Always wait until 5.00 and then bring it to me. The challenge of a deadline is always refreshing.
2. If it's really a 'rush job', run in and interrupt me every ten minutes to inquire how it's going. That greatly aids my efficiency.
3. If you give me more than one job to do, don't tell me which is the priority. Let me guess.
4. Do your best to keep me late. I like the office and really have nowhere to go or anything to do.
5. If a job I do pleases you, keep it a secret. Leaks like that could get me a promotion.
6. If you don't like my work, tell everyone.
7. If you have special instructions for a job, don't write them down. In fact, save them until the job is finished.
8. Be nice to me only when the job I'm doing for you could really change your life.
9. Tell me all your little problems. No one else has any and it's nice to know someone is less fortunate.
10. That raise you promised two years ago? I don't need it, honestly.

TEN WAYS TO MAINTAIN A HEALTHY LEVEL OF INSANITY IN THE WORKPLACE

1. Page yourself over the intercom. Don't disguise your voice.

2. Find out where your boss shops and buy exactly the same outfits. Wear them one day after your boss does. This is especially effective if your boss is of a different gender than you.

3. Send email to the rest of the company telling them exactly what you're doing. For example, 'If anyone needs me, I'll be in the bathroom.'

4. Put a chair facing a printer. Sit there all day and tell people you're waiting for your document.

5. Every time someone asks you to do something, anything, ask them if they want fries with that.

6. Send email back and forth to yourself engaging yourself in an intellectual debate. Forward the mail to a co-worker and ask her to settle the disagreement.

7. Encourage your colleagues to join you in a little synchronised chair-dancing.

8. Put your rubbish bin on your desk. Label it 'IN'.

9. Feign an unnatural and hysterical fear of staplers.

10. Bring 'special blanket' to work and carry him around in your koala bear rucksack.

FIFTEEN WAYS TO REALLY ANNOY PEOPLE IN THE OFFICE . . .

1. Learn Morse code and have conversations in meetings consisting entirely of 'Beeeep Bip Bip Beeep Bip . . .'

2. Leave the copy machine set to reduce 200 per cent, extra dark, 17 inch paper, 98 copies.

4. Sniffle incessantly.

5. Forget the punch line to a long joke, but assure your co-worker it was a 'real hoot'.

6. Do not add any inflection to the end of your sentences, producing awkward silences in meetings with the impression that you'll be saying more any moment.

7. Staple papers in the middle of the page.

8. ONLY TYPE IN UPPERCASE.
9. only type in lowercase.
10. dontuseanypunctuationeither
11. Repeat the following conversation a dozen times:
    'Do you hear that?'
    'What?'
    'Never mind, it's gone now.'
12. Stand over your boss's shoulder, mumbling, as he or she reads.
13. Lie obviously about trivial things such as the time of day.
14. Never make eye contact.
15. Never break eye contact.

FIFTEEN THINGS TO DO IN THE LIFT AT WORK

1. Grimace painfully while smacking your forehead and muttering, 'Shut up, damn it, all of you just shut UP!'
2. Whistle the first seven notes of 'It's a Small World' incessantly.
3. Crack open your briefcase or purse and while peering inside ask, 'Got enough air in there?'
4. Offer name tags to everyone getting on the elevator. Wear yours upside-down.
5. Stand silent and motionless in the corner, facing the wall, without getting off.
6. Greet everyone getting on the elevator with a warm handshake and ask them to call you Admiral.
7. Stare, grinning, at another passenger for a while and then announce, 'I've got new socks on!'
8. Meow occasionally.
9. Bet the other passengers you can fit a 50 cent coin up your nose.
10. Walk on with a cooler that says 'human head' on the side.
11. Stare at another passenger for a while, then announce 'You're one of THEM!' and move to the far corner of the elevator.
12. Wear a puppet on your hand and use it to talk to the other passengers.

13. When the elevator is silent, look around and ask, 'Is that your beeper?'
14. Say 'I wonder what all these do?' and push the red buttons.
15. Get down on your knees and start crying, 'Oh, god, my astrologer said it would end like this.'

JOB INTERVIEWS

TEN THINGS NOT TO DO IN A JOB INTERVIEW

1. Challenge the interviewer to an arm wrestle.
2. Wear a Walkman to the interview—even if you are able to listen to the interviewer and the music at the same time.
3. Trip over the mat and break your arm.
4. Eat a hamburger and French fries in the interviewer's office—even if you do explain that you did not have lunch.
5. State that your long-term goals are to replace the interviewer.
6. Claim that you never finished high school because you were kidnapped and kept in a closet in Mexico.
7. If you are balding do not excuse yourself halfway through the interview only to return wearing a hair-piece.
8. Offer to have the company logo tattooed to your forearm.
9. Phone your therapist for advice on how to answer specific interview questions.
10. Doze off during the interview.

TEN THINGS NOT TO ASK AT A JOB INTERVIEW

1. What is it that you people do at this company?
2. Why aren't you in a more interesting business?
3. What are the zodiac signs of all the board members?
4. Why do you want references?
5. Do I have to dress for the next interview?
6. I know this is off the subject, but will you marry me?
7. Would it be a problem if I'm angry most of the time?

8. Does your company have a policy regarding concealed weapons?
9. Do you think the company would be willing to lower my pay?
10. Why am I here?

Do you believe in life after death?' the boss asked one of his employees.

'Yes, sir,' the new recruit replied.

'Well, then, that makes everything just fine,' the boss went on, 'After you left early yesterday to go to your grandmother's funeral, she stopped in to see you . . .'

OFFICE TRUTHS

A pat on the back is only a few centimetres from a kick in the pants.

Don't be irreplaceable, if you can't be replaced, you can't be promoted.

The more crap you put up with, the more crap you are going to get.

You can go anywhere you want if you look serious and carry a clipboard.

Never ask two questions in a business letter. The reply will discuss the one you are least interested in and say nothing about the other.

When the bosses talk about improving productivity, they are never talking about themselves.

If at first you don't succeed, quit. No use being a damn fool about it.

There will always be beer cans rolling on the floor of your car when the boss asks for a ride home from the office.

Mother said there would be days like this, but she never said there would be so many.

MORE OFFICE TRUTHS

Everything can be filed under 'miscellaneous'.

Never delay the ending of a meeting or the beginning of a cocktail hour.

To err is human, to forgive is not company policy.

The last person that quit or was fired will be the one held responsible for everything that goes wrong—until the next person quits or is fired.

There is never enough time to do it right the first time, but there is always enough time to do it over.

You are always doing something marginal when the boss drops by your desk.

People are always available for work in the past tense.

If it weren't for the last minute, nothing would get done.

When you have nothing to do, walk fast and look worried.

You will always get the greatest recognition for the job you like least.

No one gets sick on Wednesdays.

The longer the title, the less important the job.

Machines that have broken down will work perfectly when the repairman arrives.

Success is just a matter of luck, just ask any failure.

NEW CORPORATE BUZZ WORDS

Blamestorming

Sitting around in a group discussing why a deadline was missed or a project failed and who was responsible.

Seagull Manager

A manager who flies in, makes a lot of noise and then leaves.

Chainsaw Consultant

An outside expert brought in to reduce the employee headcount, leaving the top brass with clean hands.

Cube Farm

An office filled with cubicles.

Prairie Dogging

When someone yells or drops something loudly in a Cube Farm and people's heads pop up over the walls to see what's going on.

Mouse Potato

The online, wired generation's answer to the couch potato.

SITCOMs

What yuppies turn into when they have children and one of them stops working to stay home with the kids. Stands for Single Income, Two Children, Oppressive Mortgage.

Starter Marriage

A short-lived first marriage that ends in divorce with no kids, no property and no regrets.

Stress Puppy

A person who seems to thrive on being stressed out and whiny.

Swiped Out
An ATM or credit card that has been rendered useless because the magnetic strip is worn away from extensive use.

Tourists
People who take training classes just to get a vacation from their jobs. 'We had three serious students in class; the rest were just tourists.'

Going Postal
Euphemism for being totally stressed out, for losing it. Makes reference to the unfortunate track record of postal employees who have snapped and gone on shooting rampages.

Assmosis
The process by which some people seem to absorb success and advancement by kissing up to the boss rather than working hard.

Irritainment

Entertainment and media spectacles that are annoying, but you find yourself unable to stop watching them. The life and times of Paris Hilton is a prime example.

Uninstalled

Euphemism for being fired. Heard on the voicemail of a Vice President at a downsizing computer firm: 'You have reached the number of an uninstalled Vice President. Please dial our main number and ask the operator for assistance.'

OFFICE QUOTES . . .

'We are going to continue having these meetings, everyday, until I find out why no work is getting done.'

'I didn't say it was your fault. I said I was going to blame it on you.'

'We passed over a lot of good people to get the ones we hired.'

'The beatings will continue until morale improves.'

'What you see as a glass ceiling, I see as a protective barrier.'

'I'll thump the next prick who says I'm aggressive.'

MY BOSS . . .

My boss needs a surge protector. That way his mouth would be buffered from surprise spikes in his brain.

My boss often gets lost in his own thoughts. It is because it is such unfamiliar territory.

I thought my boss was an idiot. So I quit my job to work for myself. My new boss is an idiot, too . . . but at least I respect him.

My boss has given automobile accident victims new hope for recovery. He walks, talks and performs rudimentary tasks, all without the benefit of a SPINE.

Some people climb the ladder of success. My boss walked under it.

LAWYERS

A doctor and a lawyer were attending a cocktail party when the doctor was approached by a man who asked advice on how to handle his stomach ulcer.

The doctor mumbled some medical advice, then turned to the lawyer and asked, 'How do you handle the situation when you are asked for advice during a social function?'

'Just send an account for such advice, that normally stops it!' replied the lawyer.

On the next morning the doctor arrived at his surgery and issued the ulcer-stricken man a $50 account.

That afternoon he received a $100 account from the lawyer . . .

A new client had just come in to see a well-regarded lawyer.
'Can you tell me how much you charge?' said the client.

'Of course,' the lawyer replied, 'I charge $200 to answer three questions!'

'Well that's a bit steep, isn't it?'

'Yes it is,' said the lawyer, 'And what's your third question?'

What's the difference between a good lawyer and a bad lawyer? A bad lawyer can let a case drag out for several years. A good lawyer can make it last even longer.

An airliner was having engine trouble and the pilot instructed the cabin crew to have the passengers take their seats and get prepared for an emergency landing.

A few minutes later, the pilot asked the flight attendants if everyone was buckled in and ready.

'All set back here, Captain,' came the reply, 'Except one lawyer who is still going around passing out business cards.'

When the man in the street says, 'If it ain't broke, don't fix it,' the lawyer writes,

'Insofar as manifestations of functional deficiencies are agreed by any and all concerned parties to be unperceivable and are so stipulated, it is incumbent upon said heretofore mentioned parties to exercise the deferment of otherwise pertinent maintenance procedures.'

A defending attorney was cross-examining a coroner.

The attorney asked, 'Before you signed the death certificate had you taken the man's pulse?'

'No,' the coroner replied.

The attorney then asked, 'Did you listen for a heart beat?'

The coroner said, 'No.'

'Did you check for breathing?' asked the attorney.

Again the coroner replied, 'No.'

The attorney asked, 'So when you signed the death certificate you had not taken any steps to make sure the man was dead, had you?'

The coroner, now tired of the brow beating said, 'Well, let me put it this way. The man's brain was sitting in a jar on my desk, but for all I know he could be out there practicing law somewhere.'

A young lawyer was defending a wealthy businessman in a complicated lawsuit. Unfortunately, the evidence was against his client and he feared the worst. So the lawyer asked the senior partner of the law firm if it would be appropriate to send the judge a box of Havana cigars.

The partner was horrified. 'The judge is an honourable man,' the partner exclaimed. 'If you do that, I can guarantee you will lose the case!'

Weeks later the judge ruled in favour of the lawyer's client.

The partner took him to lunch to congratulate him. 'Aren't you glad you didn't send those cigars to the judge?' the partner asked.

'But I did send them,' replied the lawyer. 'I just enclosed the plaintiff's lawyer's business card!'

A Sydney man was forced to take a day off from work to appear for a minor traffic summons. He grew increasingly restless as he waited hour after endless hour for his case to be heard.

When his name was called late in the afternoon, he stood before the judge, only to hear that court would be adjourned for the day and he would have to return the next day.

'What for?' he snapped at the judge.

His Honour, equally irked by a tedious day and sharp query roared, 'Twenty dollars contempt of court. That's why!'

Then, noticing the man checking his wallet, the judge relented. 'That's all right. You don't have to pay now.'

The man replied, 'I'm just seeing if I have enough for two more words.'

An engineer dies and reports to hell. Pretty soon the engineer, dissatisfied with the level of comfort in hell, starts designing and building improvements.

After a while, they've got air conditioning and flush toilets and escalators and the engineer is a pretty popular guy.

One day God calls Satan up on the telephone and says with a sneer, 'So, how's it going down there in Hell?'

Satan replies, 'Hey things are going great. We've got air conditioning and flush toilets and escalators and there's no telling what this engineer is going to come up with next.'

God replies, 'What? You've got an engineer? That's a mistake— he should never have gotten down there; send him up here.'

Satan says, 'No way. I like having an engineer on the staff and I'm keeping him.'

God says, 'Send him back up here or I'll sue.'

Satan laughs uproariously and answers, 'Yeah, right. And just where are you going to get a lawyer?'

LIFE'S TOUGH

Dean saw an advertisement for a blow up doll called Life-like Tina that claimed she was 'So realistic you cannot tell the difference!'

As Dean had not had a girlfriend for a long time he ordered one and waited in anticipation.

The supplier got the order from Dean. The bloke who mailed the order cannot believe how realistic 'Life-like Tina' looks. When no one is around he decides to blow it up. He then figures that seeing it is inflated he may as well give it a bit of test run. He has sex with the doll, meticulously washes it afterwards, packages it up and posts it out to Dean.

A month later Dean rings up the supplier.

'You know that 'Life-like Tina' blow up doll? I cannot tell you how happy I am.'

'That's great!' says the supplier.

'It was a totally unbelievable experience,' enthuses Dean.

'Realistic then?' asked the supplier.

'Yeah, so fucking realistic, I got syphilis . . .'

The blonde had long been infatuated with a popular local disc jockey and finally got to meet him when the station held an open house.

He seductively suggests they get better acquainted and leads her into a vacant studio where he unzips his pants.

'I suppose you know what this is?' he whispers.

'I sure do,' she says, grasping it in her hand and putting it near her mouth, 'I'd like to say hello to Ricky, Bobby, Tina and the whole gang down at Danny's Pizzeria.'

Frank came home from school one day with a note from his teacher.

It read, 'Frank seems to be having some difficulty with the differences between boys and girls. Please sit down and have a talk with Frank about this.'

So Frank's mother took him quietly by the hand, upstairs to her bedroom and closed the door.

'First, Frank, I want you to take off my blouse . . .' his mother asked.

Frank unbuttoned her blouse and took it off.

'Ok, now take off my skirt . . .'

Frank dutifully took off her skirt.

'Now take off my bra . . .'

Frank fumbled with the straps but managed to take off her bra.

'And now, Frankie, please take off my panties.'

When Frank finishes removing these, she says, 'Frank, please don't wear any of my clothes to school any more!'

Three men die in a car accident on Christmas Eve. They all find themselves at the Pearly Gates waiting to enter heaven.

Here, St Peter greets them and tells them that if they wish to enter into heaven, then they must present 'something Christmassy'. The first man searches his pockets and finds some pine needles from the family's Christmas tree.

He is let it in.

The second man presents a bow and some ribbon, from presents that were opened earlier that night.

So he is also allowed in.

The third man pulls out a pair of black lace panties.

Confused at this last gesture, St Peter says in a booming voice, 'I fail to see the relevance. How do these represent Christmas?'

To which the third man replies, 'Well . . . they're Carol's.'

Many years after Bill Clinton had been President of the United States, a famous biographer was interviewing him.

'Bill, what was your best and your worst decision during the Presidency?' he asked.

Bill thought deeply and then said, 'Monica Lewinsky! I'd have to say Monica was my best and my worst decision.'

'How could that be?' asked the surprised biographer.

Bill smiled and then shook his head, 'I'd have to say she was both my best and my worst decision for the same reason.'

'And what was that reason?' said the biographer.

Bill squirmed in his chair and answered, 'Monica had a big mouth.'

A married couple was on holiday in Pakistan when they went to a marketplace.

In the far corner of the marketplace was a dimly lit stall, with a wizened old man sitting out the front of it. As they walked past he implored them to come into his shop to see his special sandals.

'These sandals,' he said 'have magic powers. They make the wearer wild about sex, like a great desert camel.'

The wife was intrigued but the husband, who believed himself to be the world's greatest lover, was disbelieving.

'I tell you it is true,' said the old Pakistani man. 'Try them on for yourself!'

Reluctantly the man tried on the sandals. As soon as his feet slipped into the shoes he got this wild look in his eyes—a look his wife hadn't seen in many years.

Frenzied by his raw sexual power the husband rushed the Pakistani man, threw him on a table and started tearing at the guy's pants.

All the time the Pakistani man was screaming,

'You have them on the wrong feet! You have them on the wrong feet!'

The Seven Dwarfs go to the Vatican and are granted an audience with the Pope.

'Dopey, my son,' says the Pope. 'What can I do for you?'

Dopey asks, 'Excuse me, Your Excellency, but are there any dwarf nuns in Rome?'

The Pope wrinkles his brow at this odd question, thinks for a minute and answers, 'No Dopey there are no dwarf nuns in Rome.'

In the background a few of the dwarfs start sniggering. Dopey turns around and gives them a glare, silencing them.

Dopey turns back, 'Your Worship, are there any dwarf nuns in all of Europe?'

The Pope, puzzled now, again thinks for a moment and then answers, 'No Dopey, there are no dwarf nuns in Europe.'

The other dwarfs begin to giggle.

Dopey implores the Pope, 'Mr Pope, are there any dwarf nuns anywhere in the world?'

'I'm sorry, my son, there are no dwarf nuns anywhere in the world.'

The other dwarfs collapse into a heap, rolling around laughing, pounding the floor, tears rolling down their cheeks as they begin chanting . . .

'Dopey screwed a penguin! Dopey screwed a penguin!'

MATHS AND PHYSICS

There are three kinds of mathematicians:
Those who can count and those who can't . . .

A mathematician wandered home at 3 am.
His wife became very upset, telling him, 'You're late! You said you'd be home by 11.45! It's three o'clock!'

The mathematician replied, 'I'm right on time. I said I'd be home by a quarter of twelve . . .'

An engineer, a physicist, a mathematician and a mystic were asked to name the greatest invention of all times.

The engineer chose fire, which gave humanity power over matter.

The physicist chose the wheel, which gave humanity power over space.

The mathematician chose the alphabet, which gave humanity power over symbols.

The mystic chose the thermos bottle.

'Why a thermos bottle?' the others asked.

'Because the thermos keeps hot liquids hot in winter and cold liquids cold in summer.'

'Yes, so what?

'Think about it,' said the mystic reverently. 'That little bottle— how does it know?'

A physics professor, after quite some experimentation, comes up with an empirical equation to explain his data.

He asks his friend, a math professor, to look at it.

A week later, the math professor says the equation is invalid.

By then the physics professor has used his equation to predict the results of further experiments and is getting excellent results. So he asks the math professor to look again.

Another week goes by and they meet once more. The math professor tells the physics professor the equation does work, 'But only in the trivial case where the numbers are real and positive . . .'

The experimentalist comes running excitedly into the theorist's office, waving a graph taken off his latest experiment.

'Hmmm,' says the theorist, 'That's exactly where you'd expect to see that peak. Here's the reason.'

A long logical explanation follows.

In the middle of it, the experimentalist says, 'Wait a minute', studies the chart for a second and says, 'Oops, this is upside down.'

He fixes it.

'Hmmm,' says the theorist, 'You'd expect to see a dip in exactly that position. Here's the reason . . .'

A farmer has problems with his chickens. For no apparent reason, they have become very sick and are dying.

After trying all conventional means, he calls a physicist to see if she can figure out what is wrong.

The physicist comes to the farm and stands looking at the chickens for a long time without saying anything.

Suddenly, she starts scribbling away in a notebook.

Finally, after several pages of calculations, she exclaims, 'I've got it! But it only works for spherical chickens in a vacuum.'

A physicist, biologist and a chemist went to the ocean for the first time.

The physicist saw the ocean and was fascinated by the waves. He said he wanted to do some research on the fluid dynamics of the waves and walked into the ocean. He was never seen again.

The biologist said he wanted to do research on the flora and fauna inside the ocean and walked into the ocean. He too, never returned.

The chemist waited for a long time and afterwards, wrote the observation, 'The physicist and the biologist are soluble in ocean water'.

A mathematician, a physicist and an engineer were all given a red rubber ball and told to find the volume.

The mathematician carefully measured the diameter and evaluated a triple integral.

The physicist filled a beaker with water, put the ball in the water and measured the total displacement.

The engineer looked up the model and serial numbers in his Red-Rubber-Ball Table.

What's the difference between mechanical engineers and civil engineers?

Mechanical engineers build weapons.

Civil engineers build targets.

MEDIA MADNESS

An advertising team is working very late at night on a project due the next morning. Suddenly, a Genie appears before them and offers to each of them one wish.

The copywriter says, 'I've always dreamed of writing the great American novel and having my work studied in schools across the land. I'd like to go to a tropical island where I can concentrate and write my masterpiece.'

The Genie says, 'No problem!' and poof! The copywriter is gone.

The art director says, 'I want to create a painting so beautiful that it would hang in the Louvre Museum in Paris for all the world to admire. I want to go to the French countryside to work on my painting.'

The Genie says, 'Your wish is granted!' and poof! The art director is gone.

The Genie then turns to the account executive and says, 'And what is your wish?'

The account executive says, 'I want those two ass-holes back here right now.'

A photographer for a national magazine was assigned to get photos of a huge bush fire. The smoke at the scene was too thick to get any good shots, so he frantically called his home office to hire a plane.

'It will be waiting for you at the airport!' he was assured by his editor.

As soon as he got to the small, rural airport, sure enough, a plane was warming up near the runway.

He jumped in with his equipment and yelled, 'Let's go! Let's go!'

The pilot swung the plane onto the runway and soon they were in the air.

'Fly over the north side of the fire,' said the photographer, 'And make three or four low level passes.'

'Why?' asked the pilot.

'Because I'm going to take pictures! I'm a photographer and photographers take pictures!' said the photographer with great exasperation.

After a long pause the pilot said, 'You mean you're not the instructor?'

A cadet reporter for a small town newspaper was sent out on his first assignment.

He submitted the following report to his editor,

'Mrs Smith was injured in a car accident today. She is recovering in County Hospital with lacerations on her breasts.'

The Editor scolded the new reporter, 'This is a family paper. We don't use words like breasts around here. Now go back and write something more appropriate!'

The young reporter thought long and hard.

Finally he handed the editor the following report, 'Mrs Smith was injured in a car accident today. She is recovering in County Hospital with lacerations on her (.)(.)'.

A man went in for an interview for a job as a TV news broadcaster. The interview went quite well but the trouble was he kept winking and stammering.

The interviewer said, 'Although you have a lot of the qualities we're looking for, the fact that you keep winking and stammering disqualifies you.'

'Oh, that's no problem,' said the man. 'If I take a couple of aspirin, I stop winking and stammering for an hour.'

'Show me,' said the interviewer.

So the man reached into his pocket. Embarrassingly he pulled out loads of condoms of every variety—ribbed, flavoured, coloured—before he found the packet of aspirin. He took the aspirin and soon talked perfectly and stopped winking.

The interviewer said, 'That's amazing, but I don't think we could employ someone who'd be womanising all over the country.'

'Excuse me!' exclaimed the man, 'I'm a happily married man, not a womaniser!'

'Well how do you explain all the condoms, then?' asked the interviewer.

The man replied, 'Have you ever gone into a pharmacy, stammering and winking and asked for a packet of aspirin?'

There was once a young man who, in his youth, professed his desire to become a great writer.

When asked to define great, he said, 'I want to write stuff that the whole world will read, stuff that people will react to on a truly emotional level, stuff that will make them scream, cry, howl in pain and anger!'

He now works for Microsoft writing error messages.

MILITARY MINDSET

TEN THINGS TO REMEMBER IF YOU ARE EVER CONSCRIPTED

1. The only thing more accurate than enemy fire is friendly fire.
2. Try to look unimportant, they may be low on ammo.
3. Teamwork is essential. It gives them more targets to shoot at.
4. No inspection-ready unit ever passed combat.
5. No combat-ready unit ever passed inspection.
6. Remember: your aircraft was made by the lowest bidder.
7. Never share a cockpit with someone braver than you.
8. You are not Tom Cruise.
9. The best defence is to stay out of range.
10. If you are short on everything but enemy, you are in combat.

'**W**ell,' snarled the tough old Navy Chief to the bewildered Seaman. 'I suppose after you get discharged from the Navy, you'll just be waiting for me to die so you can come and piss on my grave.'

'Not me, Chief!' the Seaman replied. 'Once I get out of the Navy, I'm never going to stand in line again . . .!'

An Army Cadet was almost killed in a tragic horseback riding accident. He fell from the horse and was nearly trampled to death. Thank goodness the manager of the K-Mart came out and unplugged it.

TALK IT OUT

One reason the Defence Services have trouble operating jointly is that they don't speak the same language.

For example:

- If you told Navy personnel to 'secure a building', they would turn off the lights and lock the doors.
- Army personnel would occupy the building so no one could enter.
- Special Forces would assault the building, capture it and defend it with suppressive fire and close combat.
- The Air Force, on the other hand, would take out a three-year lease with an option to buy.

A sergeant was addressing a squad of 20 and said, 'I have a nice easy job for the laziest man here. Put up your hand if you are the laziest.'

Nineteen of the 20 men raised their hands.

The sergeant turned and asked the remaining man, 'Why didn't you raise your hand?'

The man replied, 'Too much trouble, Sarge.'

MUSICAL NOTES

What's the definition of an optimist?
A folk musician with a mortgage.

An anthropologist decided to investigate the natives of a far-flung tropical island.

He flew there, found a guide with a canoe to take him up the river to the remote site where he would make his collections. About noon on the second day of travel up the river, they began to hear drums.

Being a city boy by nature, the anthropologist was disturbed by this. He asked the guide, 'What are those drums?'

The guide turned to him and said 'Drums okay, but very bad when they stop.'

After some hours, the drums suddenly stopped!

Panicked, the anthropologist yells at the guide, 'The drums have stopped, what happens now?'

The guide crouched down, covered his head with his hands and said, 'Bass Solo.'

A couple was having marital difficulties and consulted a marriage counsellor.

After meeting with them, the counsellor told them that their problems could all be traced to a lack of communication.

'You two need to talk,' he said.

'So, I recommend that you go to a jazz club. Just wait until it is time for the bass player to solo. Then you'll be talking just like everyone else.'

What's the difference between a musician and a savings bond? One of them eventually matures and earns money.

What do you call a musician who doesn't have a girlfriend? Homeless!

Donald MacDonald from the Isle of Skye was admitted to Oxford University and was living in his first year of residence there.

His clan was very excited that one of their own had made it into the upper class of education, but were concerned how he'd do in 'that strange land'.

After the first month, his mother came to visit, with reinforcements of whisky, haggis and oatmeal.

'And how do you find the English students, Donald?' she asked.

'Oh, Mother,' he replied, shaking his head sadly, 'They're such terrible, noisy people. The one on that side incessantly bangs his head against the wall and the one on the other side screams all night.'

'But Donald! How do you manage with those dreadful noisy English neighbours?'

'Well, mother, I just ignore 'em. I just stay here quietly, playing my bagpipes . . .'

OH, NO, NOT MORE LAWYERS!

NASA was interviewing applicants to be sent to Mars. Even though it was a one way trip there was plenty of interest in the last berth aboard the spacecraft.

The first applicant, an engineer, was asked how much he wanted to be paid for going.

'A million dollars,' he answered, 'Because I want to donate it to Oxford University.'

The next applicant, a doctor, was asked the same question. He asked for $2 million.

'I want to give a million to my family,' he explained, 'And leave the other million for the advancement of medical research.'

The last applicant was a lawyer.

When asked how much money he wanted, he whispered in the interviewer's ear, 'Three million dollars.'

'Why so much more than the others?' asked the interviewer.

The lawyer replied, 'If you give me $3 million, I'll give you $1 million, I'll keep $1 million and we'll send the engineer to Mars.'

A clever attorney was convinced he had found a way to take all of his riches with him when he died.

When he realised that his death was imminent, he instructed his wife to sell all of his investments and buy gold coins with the proceeds.

She was instructed to put the gold in several bags with handles and place them in the attic directly over his bedroom.

His plan was that when he died, his soul would rise up out of his body and ascend to heaven. As he passed through the attic, he would grab the bags of gold and take them with him.

Days later he finally died and the next day his wife went to the attic to see if the gold was gone, but found it was all still there.

'The damn fool,' she said to herself. 'I told him we should have placed the bags in the basement.'

A dying man gathered his Lawyer, Doctor and Clergyman at his bedside and handed each of them an envelope containing $25,000 in cash.

He made them each promise that after his death they would place the three envelopes in his coffin. He told them that he wanted to have enough money to enjoy the next life.

A week later the man died.

At the viewing of the body the Lawyer, Doctor and Clergyman each concealed an envelope in the coffin as they had been instructed.

After the burial the three went back to the wake.

Liking a tipple, the Clergyman had soon drunk enough sherry to loosen his lips. He confessed to the other two men that the envelope he had placed in the coffin had only contained $10,000. He felt that the money would be better spent on charity work in South America.

The Doctor, moved by the Clergyman's sincerity, admitted that he too had kept some of the money. The envelope he had put in the coffin had only $8000 in it. He said he could not bring himself to waste the money so frivolously so he had donated it to medical research.

By this time the Lawyer was seething with self-righteous rage.

'I was the only one who has kept his promise!' he exploded.

'It is just lucky for you two that I wrote a personal cheque for the entire amount!'

A local charity rang the town's most successful lawyer to ask for a donation.

The lawyer started raging, 'Are you aware that my mother is sick and burdened by medical bills that are three times her annual income or that my sister's husband has recently died in an accident which has left her penniless with three children or that my brother is blind and has no money to pay for an aid or a nurse?'

'Um, sorry,' replied the man, 'I had no idea.'

Then the lawyer said 'So if I don't give any money to them, why would I give any money to you?'

Two five-year-old boys were playing together at the park.

'My name is Joshua. What's yours?' asked the first boy.

'Adam,' replied the second.

'My daddy is a doctor. What does your daddy do for a living?' asked Joshua.

Adam proudly replied, 'My daddy is a lawyer.'

'Honest?' asked Joshua.

'No, just the regular kind,' replied Adam.

Q: Why are lawyers like nuclear weapons?

A: If one side has one, the other side has to get one. Once launched, they cannot be recalled. When they land, they screw up everything forever.

A lawyer opened the door of his BMW, when suddenly a car came along and hit the door, ripping it off completely. When the police arrived at the scene, the lawyer was complaining bitterly about the damage to his precious BMW.

'Officer, look what they've done to my Beamer!' he whined.

'You lawyers are so materialistic, you make me sick!' retorted the officer.

'You're so worried about your stupid BMW, that you didn't even notice that your left arm was ripped off!'

'Oh my God!' replied the lawyer, finally noticing the bloody left shoulder where his arm once was, 'Where's my Rolex?'

A man is at his lawyer's funeral and is surprised by the turnout for this one man.

He turns to the people around him, 'How did you know this man?'

A man turns towards him and says, 'We're all clients.'

'And you ALL came to pay your respects? How touching.'

'No, we came to make sure the bastard was dead.'

DIRTY LAWYER SAYINGS

1. Have you looked through her briefs?
2. He is one hard judge!
3. Her attorney withdrew at the last minute.
4. For $200 an hour, she better be good!
5. Can you get him to drop his suit?
6. Think you can get me off?

A man was sent to Hell for his sins.
As he was being taken to his place of eternal torment he passed a room where a lawyer was having an intimate encounter with a beautiful young woman.

'What a rip-off,' the man muttered. 'I have to push large boulders up a hill for the rest of eternity and that lawyer gets to spend it with a beautiful woman.'

Jabbing the man with his pitchfork, the escorting demon snarled, 'Who are you to question that woman's punishment?'

One day a truck driver was driving along when he noticed a priest whose car had broken down.

He pulled over and offered the priest a lift to the next town to get help.

As they approached the town they drove past the courthouse.

Now, the truck-driver had been through a messy divorce and hated lawyers. So he had made it a practice to hit any pedestrian lawyers with his truck as he sped by.

The truck driver saw a lawyer walking out of the courthouse. Automatically, he veered his truck towards the lawyer, but he then remembered his ecclesiastical passenger.

He swerved back to the centre of the road to avoid hitting the lawyer.

Yet he heard a large bang and when he looked in the rear vision mirror he saw the lawyer lying on the road.

He turned to the priest and said, 'Father, I'm sure that I missed that lawyer!'

The priest replied, 'That's okay, my son, I got him with the door.'

ON THE LAND

There was a farmer who grew watermelons.

Every week he would come to check on his crop and would find that the local kids had gotten into his field and eaten as many watermelons as they could.

This went on for quite some time and the man eventually got fed up at having to replant the missing watermelons.

After some careful thought he came up with a clever idea that he thought would scare the kids away for sure.

He made up a sign and posted it in the field.

It read ominously, 'Warning! One of the watermelons in this field has been injected with cyanide.' He is very pleased with himself and is sure that when he next checks on his crop there will be no watermelons missing.

A couple of days later the farmer returns to his field. He is pleased to find that no watermelons are missing, although in the distance he can see something next to the sign he has posted. He walks over to it to see another sign that says, 'Now there are two'.

An efficiency consultant employed in the farming sector went out to evaluate work practices in an orchard.

After several days of close analysis he reported back to the farmer, 'Your methods are too old fashioned. You need to update your work practices and supply chain if you are to increase your yield. For example, I wouldn't be surprised if this tree will give you less than ten kilograms of apples.'

Said the farmer 'I won't be surprised either . . . this is an orange tree.'

ONE-UPMANSHIP

The Americans and the Japanese decided to engage in a competitive boat race. Both teams practised hard and long to reach their peak performance.

On the big day the Japanese won by a mile.

The American team was discouraged by the loss. Morale sagged. Corporate management decided that the reason for the crushing defeat had to be found, so a consulting firm was hired to investigate the problem and recommend corrective action.

The consultant's findings were as follows:

The Japanese team had eight people rowing and one person steering; the American team had one person rowing and eight people steering.

After a year of study and millions of dollars spent analysing the problem, the American team's management structure was completely reorganised.

The new structure was four steering managers, three area steering managers and a new performance review system for the person rowing the boat to provide work incentive.

The next year, the Japanese won by two miles!

Humiliated, the American corporation laid off the rower for poor performance and gave the managers a bonus for discovering the problem.

A CEO was throwing a large party and was taking his executives on a tour of his opulent mansion.

At the back of the property was the largest swimming pool any of them had ever seen. The huge pool, however, was filled with hungry crocodiles.

The CEO said to his executives 'I think an executive should be measured by courage. Courage is what made me CEO.

'So this is my challenge to each of you—if anyone has enough courage to dive into the pool, swim through those crocodiles and make it to the other side, I will give that person anything they desire.'

Everyone laughed at the outrageous offer and continued on with the tour of the estate.

Suddenly, they heard a loud splash. Everyone turned around and saw the Chief Financial Officer in the pool, swimming for his life.

He dodged the crocodiles left and right and made it to the edge of the pool with seconds to spare.

The flabbergasted CEO approached the CFO and said, 'You are amazing. I've never seen anything like it in my life. You are brave beyond measure and anything I own is yours. Tell me what I can do for you.'

The CFO, panting for breath, looked up and said, 'You can tell me who the hell pushed me in the pool!'

MANAGEMENT RULES

- The first myth of management is that it exists.
- Some people manage by the book, even though they don't know who wrote the book or even what book.
- We are too busy mopping the floor to turn off the tap.
- Management by objectives is no better than the objectives.
- 'I've given you an unlimited budget and you have already exceeded it!'

A physician, a civil engineer and a consultant were arguing about what was the oldest profession in the world.

The physician remarked, 'Well, in the Bible, it says that God created Eve from a rib taken out of Adam. This clearly required surgery and so I can rightly claim that mine is the oldest profession in the world.'

The civil engineer interrupted and said, 'But even earlier in the book of Genesis, it states that God created the order of the heavens and the earth from out of the chaos. This was the first and certainly the most spectacular application of civil engineering. Therefore, you are wrong—mine is the oldest profession in the world.'

The consultant leaned back in her chair, smiled and then said confidently, 'Ah, but who do you think created the chaos?'

The classified ad read, 'Wanted: CEO needs a one armed consultant, with a social sciences degree and five years of experience.'

The man who won the job asked, 'I understood most of the qualifications you required, but why did you want me to be one armed?'

The CEO answered, 'I have had many consultants and I am tired of hearing, with every piece of advice offered, the phrase "on the other hand".'

An efficiency expert concluded his lecture with a note of caution. 'Don't try these techniques at home.'

'Why not?' asked somebody from the audience.

'I watched my wife's routine at breakfast for years,' the expert explained.

'She made lots of trips between the fridge, stove, table and bench, often carrying a single item at a time. One day I told her, 'You're wasting too much time. Why don't you try carrying several things at once?'

'Did it save time?' a man in the audience asked.

'Actually, yes,' replied the expert. 'It used to take her 20 minutes to make breakfast. Now I do it in ten.'

The chickens in a large hen house had become agitated and were pecking each other to death at an alarming rate.

The farmer tried several things but the chickens still continued to fight and kill each other. So the farmer hired a consultant to solve his problem.

'Add baking-powder to the chickens' food,' said the consultant, 'It will calm them down.'

After a week the farmer came back to the consultant and said, 'It's no good. My chickens continue to die. What should I do?'

'Add strawberry juice to their drinking water, that will help for sure.'

A week passed and again the farmer came to the consultant, 'My chickens are still fighting. Do you have some more advice?'

'I can give you more and more advice,' answered the consultant. 'The real question is whether you have more chickens.'

A priest, a rabbi and a consultant were travelling on an aeroplane.

There was a large bang and it was soon clear that the plane was going to crash and they would all be killed.

The priest began to pray and finger his rosary beads.

The rabbi began to read the Torah.

The consultant began to organise a committee on air traffic safety.

TOP TEN THINGS YOU'LL NEVER HEAR FROM A CONSULTANT

1. You're right; you are paying me way too much for this.
2. Bet you I can go a week without saying 'synergy' or 'value-added'.
3. How about paying us based on the success of the project?
4. This whole strategy is based on a Harvard business case I read.
5. Actually, the only difference is that we charge more than they do.
6. I don't know enough to speak intelligently about that.
7. Implementation? I only care about writing long reports.
8. I can't take the credit. It was Ed in your Marketing Department.
9. The problem is, you have too much work for too few people.
10. Everything looks okay to me. You really don't need me.

Two biologists are in the field following the tracks of a radio-collared grizzly bear. Suddenly, the bear crashes out of the bush and heads right for them. They scramble up the nearest tree, but the bear starts climbing up the tree after them.

The first biologist starts taking off his heavy leather hiking boots and pulls a pair of sleek running shoes from his backpack.

The second biologist gives him a puzzled look and says, 'What in the world are you doing?'

He replies, 'I figure when the bear gets close to us, we'll jump down and make a run for it.'

The second guy says, 'Are you crazy? We both know you can't outrun a full-grown grizzly bear.'

ADULTS ONLY OFFICE JOKES

The first guy says, 'I don't have to outrun the bear, I only have to outrun you!'

A doctor, an engineer and a fungal taxonomist arrived at The Pearly Gates.

The doctor said how he'd healed the sick and helped the lame; but he was a sinner and so was sent to Hell.

The engineer claimed he had built homes for the homeless and dispossessed; but he had messed up the environment while doing it and so he was sent to Hell.

The fungal taxonomist was frightened by all this, but as soon as he mentioned his occupation, God said 'You've already been through Hell, welcome to Heaven.'

A businessman phones his wife from his office and says, 'Honey, something has just come up, I realise I'm not due in London for another few months but I have to fly there to sort out some complications.

'So, would you pack my clothes, my lap-top and my favourite blue silk pyjamas? I'll be home soon to pick them up.'

A week later he returned.

'Did you have a good trip, dear?' his wife asked.

'Oh, it was just a business trip, you know, work, work, work, I was at the computer all the time,' he exclaimed and added, 'But you forgot to pack my blue silk pyjamas.'

'No I didn't,' she replied. 'I put them with your laptop!'

A biologist was interested in studying how far bullfrogs can jump. He brought a bullfrog into his laboratory, set it down and commanded, 'Jump, frog, jump!'

The frog jumped across the room.

The biologist measured the distance, then noted in his journal, 'Frog with four legs jumped eight feet.'

136 • ADULTS ONLY OFFICE JOKES

Then he cut the frog's front legs off. Again he ordered, 'Jump, frog, jump!'

The frog struggled a moment, then jumped a few feet.

After measuring the distance, the biologist noted in his journal, 'Frog with two legs jumped three feet.'

Next, the biologist cut off the frog's back legs. Once more, he shouted, 'Jump, frog, jump!'

The frog just lay there.

'Jump, frog, jump!' the biologist repeated.

Nothing.

The biologist noted in his journal, 'Frog with no legs—lost its hearing.'

Two accountants are in a bank, when armed robbers burst in. While several of the robbers take the money from the tellers, others line the customers up against a wall and proceed to take their wallets and valuables.

While this is going on the first accountant jams something into the other's hand.

Without looking down, the second accountant whispers, 'What is this?'

The first replies, 'It's that $50 I owe you.'

A doctor is to give a speech at the local AMA dinner, so he jots down notes for his speech.

Unfortunately, when he stands in front of his colleagues later that night, he finds that he can't read his notes.

So he asks, 'Is there a pharmacist in the house?'

An accountant is having a hard time sleeping and goes to see his doctor. 'Doctor, I just can't get to sleep at night.'

'Have you tried counting sheep?'

'That's the problem—I make a mistake and then spend three hours trying to find it.'

A young accountant spends a week at his new office with the retiring accountant he is replacing.

Each and every morning the more experienced accountant begins the day by opening his desk drawer, taking out a worn envelope and removing a yellowing sheet of paper.

He reads it, nods his head, looks around the room with renewed vigour, returns the envelope to the drawer and then begins his day's work.

After he retires, the new accountant can hardly wait to read for himself the message contained in the envelope in the drawer.

Surely, he thinks to himself, it must contain the great secret to his success, a wondrous treasure of inspiration and motivation.

His fingers tremble anxiously as he removes the mysterious envelope from the drawer and reads the following message, 'Debits in the column towards the file cabinet.

Credits in the column towards the window.'

BUSINESS TRUISMS

- Budget is an orderly system for living beyond your means.
- The opulence of the front office decor varies inversely with the fundamental solvency of the firm.
- For every tax problem there is a solution which is straightforward, uncomplicated and wrong.

PASS THE ANAESTHETIC

A man has a heart attack and is brought to the hospital ER. The doctor tells him that he will not live unless he has a heart transplant right away.

Another doctor runs into the room and says, 'You're in luck, two hearts just became available, so you will get to choose which one you want. One belongs to an attorney and the other to a social worker.'

The man quickly responds, 'The attorney's.'

The doctor says, 'Wait! Don't you want to know a little about them before you make your decision?'

The man says, 'I already know enough. We all know that social workers are bleeding hearts and the attorney's probably never used his. So I'll take the attorney's!'

A man goes to his doctor for a complete check-up. He hasn't been feeling well and wants to find out if he's ill. After the check-up the doctor comes out with the results of the examination.

'I'm afraid I have some bad news. You're dying and you don't have much time,' the doctor says.

'Oh no, that's terrible. How long have I got?' the man asks.

'Ten . . .' says the doctor.

'Ten? Ten what? Months? Weeks? What?' he asks desperately.

'Ten . . . nine . . . eight . . . seven . . .'

A man went to see his doctor because he was suffering from a miserable cold. His doctor prescribed some pills, but they didn't help.

On his next visit the doctor gave him a shot, but that didn't do any good.

On his third visit the doctor told the man, 'Go home and take a hot bath. As soon as you finish bathing, throw open all the windows and stand in the draft.'

'But doc,' protested the patient, 'If I do that, I'll get pneumonia.'

'I know,' said the doctor, 'I can cure pneumonia.'

A guy walks into work and both of his ears are all bandaged up. The boss says, 'What happened to your ears?'

He says, 'Yesterday I was ironing a shirt when the phone rang and I accidentally answered the iron.'

The boss says, 'Well, that explains one ear, but what happened to your other ear?'

He says, 'Well, jeez, I had to call the doctor!'

SHORT HISTORY OF MEDICINE

'Doctor, I have an ear ache.'

2000 BC   'Here, eat this root.'
1000 BC   'That root is heathen, say this prayer.'
1850 AD   'That prayer is superstition, drink this potion.'
1940 AD   'That potion is snake oil, swallow this pill.'
1985 AD   'That pill is ineffective, take this antibiotic.'
2000 AD   'That antibiotic is artificial. Here, eat this root!'

A pipe burst in a doctor's house. He called a plumber.

The plumber arrived, unpacked his tools, did mysterious plumber-type things for a while and handed the doctor a bill for $600.

The doctor exclaimed, 'This is ridiculous! I don't even make that much as a doctor!.'

The plumber quietly answered, 'Neither did I when I was a doctor.'

A doctor said to his car mechanic, 'Your pay is several times more per hour then we get paid for medical care.'

'Yeah, but you see, doc, you have always the same model, it hasn't changed since Adam; but we have to keep up to date with new models coming every year.'

The seven-year-old girl told her mum, 'A boy in my class asked me to play doctor.'

'Oh, dear,' the mother nervously sighed. 'What happened, honey?'

'Nothing, he made me wait 45 minutes and then double-billed the insurance company.'

A veterinarian was feeling ill and went to see her doctor. The doctor began to ask her all the usual questions—her symptoms, how long had they been occurring, her lifestyle and had just asked about her bowel motions when she interrupted him.

'Hey look, I'm a vet. I don't need to ask my patients these kind of questions. I can tell what's wrong just by looking. Why can't you?'

The doctor nodded, looked her up and down, wrote out a prescription and handed it to her and said, 'There you are. Of course, if that doesn't work, we'll have to have you put down.'

A fellow walked into a doctor's office and the receptionist asked him what he had.

He said, 'Shingles.'

So she took down his name, address, medical insurance number and told him to have a seat.

A few minutes later a nurse's aid came out and asked him what he had.

He said, 'Shingles.'

So she took down his height, weight, a complete medical history and told him to wait in the examining room.

Ten minutes later a nurse came in and asked him what he had.

He said, 'Shingles.'

So she gave him a blood test, a blood pressure test, an electrocardiogram, told him to take off all his clothes and wait for the doctor.

Fifteen minutes later the doctor came in and asked him what he had.

He said, 'Shingles.'

The doctor said, 'Where?'

He said, 'Outside in the truck. Where do you want them?'

A woman, calling Melbourne Hospital, said, 'Hello, I want to know if a patient is getting better.'

The voice on the other end of the line said, 'What is the patient's name and room number?'

She said, 'She's Sarah Williams, in Room 302.'

He said, 'Oh, yes. Mrs Williams is doing very well. In fact, she's had two full meals, her blood pressure is fine, she's going to be taken off the heart monitor in a couple of hours and if she continues this improvement, Dr Cohen is going to send her home Tuesday.'

The woman said, 'Thank god! That's wonderful! Oh! That's fantastic! That's wonderful news!'

The man on the phone said, 'From your enthusiasm, I take it you must be a close family member or a very close friend!'

She said, 'I'm Sarah Williams in 302! Cohen, my doctor, doesn't tell me a word!'

If it is dry—moisten;
If it is moist—dry.

Congratulations, now you are a dermatologist.

What's the difference between a general practitioner and a specialist?

One treats what you have, the other thinks you have what he treats.

An executive had a stress induced heart attack and was taken to the hospital.

While on the operating table she had a near death experience.

Seeing God she asked, 'Is my time up?'

God answered, 'No, you have another 40 years, two months and eight days to live.'

When she recovered from the anaesthetic, she was very pleased at her new lease of life. Since she had so much more time to live, she figured she might as well make the most of it.

So she decided to stay in the hospital and have a facelift, liposuction and a tummy tuck. She even had someone come in and change her hair colour.

After her last operation, she was released from the hospital.

While crossing the street on her way home, she was hit by a car and died immediately.

Arriving in front of God, she demanded, 'I thought you said I had another 40 years, why didn't you pull me from out of the path of the car?'

God replied, 'I didn't recognise you.'

THINGS YOU DON'T WANT TO HEAR DURING SURGERY

1. Oops!
2. That was some party last night. I can't remember when I've been that drunk.
3. Damn! Page 47 of the manual is missing!
4. Better save that. We'll need it for the autopsy.
5. Come back with that! Bad Dog!
6. Wait a minute, if this is his spleen, then what's that?
7. Hand me that . . . uh . . . that uh . . . thingy.
8. Sterile, shhh-merile. The floor's clean, right?
9. This patient has already had some kids, am I correct?
10. Don't worry. I think it's sharp enough.
11. Hey Charlie, unzip the bag on that one, he's still moving.

At a medical convention, a male doctor and a female doctor catch each other's eye.

Eventually the male doctor summons the courage to ask her out to dinner and she gladly accepts.

As they sit down at the restaurant, she excuses herself to go and wash her hands.

The dinner goes exceedingly well. They both have a lot in common, and heady with champagne they end up in her hotel bedroom.

Just as things get hot, the female doctor interrupts and says she has to go and wash her hands.

The man is a little perturbed and is even more so when she

goes to wash her hands again straight after they finish making love.

As she comes back the male doctor says, 'I bet you are a surgeon'.

She confirms and asks how he knew.

'Easy, you're always washing your hands.'

She then says, 'I bet you're an anaesthesiologist.'

The male doctor is impressed, 'Wow, how did you guess?'

'I didn't feel a thing.'

PROFESSIONS

- Old accountants never die, they just lose their balance.
- Old actuaries never die, they just get broken down by age and sex.
- Old chemists never die, they just fail to react.
- Old cosmologists never die, they just go to another world.
- Old doctors never die, they just lose their patience.
- Old electricians never die, they just lose their spark.
- Old lawyers never die, they just threaten their doctor with malpractice.
- Old mathematicians never die, they just lose some of their functions.
- Old professors never die, they just lose their faculties.
- Old programmers never die, they just branch to a new address.
- Old publishers never die, they just go out of print.
- Old statisticians never die, they just become insignificant.
- Old soldiers never die. Young ones do.

A LIGHT PLANE HAS LOST POWER AND IS ABOUT TO CRASH. THERE IS ONLY ONE PARACHUTE. HOW WOULD YOU REACT IF YOU WERE A . . .

Bureaucrat: You order them to conduct a feasibility study on parachute use in multi-engine aircraft under code red conditions.

Computer Scientist: You design a machine capable of operating a parachute as well as a human being could.

Mathematician: You refuse to accept the parachute without proof that it will work in all cases.

Engineer: You make them another parachute out of aisle curtains and dental floss.

Psychoanalyst: You ask them what the shape of a parachute reminds them of.

Doctor: You tell them you need to run more tests, then take the parachute in order to make your next appointment.

Lawyer: You charge one parachute for helping them sue the airline.

Judge: After reminding them of their constitutional right to have a parachute, you take it and jump out.

Economist:	Your only rational and moral choice is to take the parachute, as the free market will take care of the other person.
Statistician:	You plot a demand curve by asking them, at regular intervals, how much they would pay for a parachute.
Manager:	As you jump out with the parachute, you tell them to work hard and not expect handouts.
Consultant:	You tell them not to worry, since it won't take you long to learn how to fix a plane.
Salesperson:	You sell them the parachute at top retail rates and get the names of their friends and relatives who might like one too.
Advertiser:	You strip-tease while singing that what they need is a neon parachute with computer altimeter for only $39.99.
Philosopher:	You ask how they know the parachute actually exists.
Modern Painter:	You hang the parachute on the wall and sign it.
Auto Mechanic:	As long as you are looking at the plane engine, it works fine.

DEFINITIONS

An accountant is someone who knows the cost of everything and the value of nothing.

An actuary is someone who brings a fake bomb on a plane, because that decreases the chances that there will be another bomb on the plane.

An archaeologist is a person whose career lies in ruins.

An architect is someone who makes beautiful models, but unaffordable realities.

An auditor is someone who arrives after the battle and bayonets all the wounded.

A banker is a fellow who lends you his umbrella when the sun is shining and wants it back the minute it begins to rain.

A consultant is someone who takes the watch off your wrist and tells you the time.

A diplomat is someone who can tell you to go to hell in such a way that you will look forward to the trip.

An economist is an expert who will know tomorrow why the things he predicted yesterday didn't happen today.

A journalist is someone who spends 50 per cent of his time not saying what he knows and 50 per cent of his time talking about things he doesn't know.

A lawyer is a person who writes a 10,000 word document and calls it a 'brief.'

A mathematician is a blind man in a dark room looking for a black cat which isn't there.

A modern artist is one who throws paint on canvas, wipes it off with a cloth and sells the cloth.

A philosopher is a person who doesn't have a job, but at least understands why.

A professor is someone who talks in someone else's sleep.

A programmer is someone who solves a problem you didn't know you had in a way you don't understand.

A psychologist is a man to whom you pay a lot of money to ask you questions that your wife asks free of charge.

A schoolteacher is a disillusioned woman who used to think she liked children.

A sociologist is someone who, when a beautiful woman enters the room and everybody look at her, looks at everybody.

A statistician is someone who is good with numbers but lacks the personality to be an accountant.

AN EFFICIENCY CONSULTANT'S CRITIQUE OF SCHUBERT'S UNFINISHED SYMPHONY

1. All 12 violins played the same notes. This is unnecessary duplication. Their number should be reduced.
2. For a considerable period, the oboe players had nothing to do.

Their number should be reduced and their work spread evenly among other staff.

3. No useful purpose is served by repeating with horns the passage that was already handled by the strings. If such redundancies were eliminated, the concert could be cut by 20 minutes.

4. The symphony has two movements. Mr Schubert should have been able to achieve his musical goals in one.

Conclusion: If Mr Schubert had paid attention to these matters, he would have had time to finish the symphony.

UNIVERSITY MEMO

From: The Dean
To: Physics Department

I have been reviewing budgets for the next financial year. It has come to my attention that the physics department has one of the largest budgetary needs, particularly for the maintenance of the laboratories and the need for expensive equipment.

Why can't you be like the math department? All they need is money for pencils, paper and waste-paper baskets.

Or even better, like the philosophy department. All they need are pencils and paper.

—The Dean.

The First Law of Philosophy:
For every philosopher, there exists an equal and opposite philosopher.

The Second Law of Philosophy:
They're both wrong.

The French existentialist Jean-Paul Sartre was sitting in a cafe when a waitress approached him, 'Can I get you something to drink, Monsieur Sartre?'

Sartre replied, 'Yes, I'd like a cup of coffee with sugar, but no cream.'

Nodding agreement, the waitress walked off to fill the order and Sartre returned to work.

A few minutes later, however, the waitress returned and said, 'I'm sorry, Monsieur Sartre, we are all out of cream, how about with no milk?'

A nun is undressing for a bath and while she's standing naked, there's a knock at the door.

The nun calls, 'Who is it?'

A voice answers, 'A blind salesman.'

The nun decides to get a thrill by having the blind man in the room while she's naked so she lets him in.

The man walks in, looks straight at the nun and says, 'Uh, well hello there, can I sell you a blind, dearie . . .?'

The manager of a large city zoo was drafting a letter to order a pair of animals.

He sat at his computer and typed the following sentence, 'I would like to place an order for two mongooses, to be delivered at your earliest convenience'.

He stared at the screen, focusing on that odd word, mongooses.

Then he deleted the word and added another, so that the sentence now read: 'I would like to place an order for two mongeeses to be delivered at your earliest convenience.'

Again he stared at the screen, this time focusing on the new word, which seemed just as odd as the original one.

Finally, he deleted the whole sentence and started all over. 'Everyone knows no full-stocked zoo should be without a mongoose,' he typed. 'Please send us two of them.'

A blonde has been sent overseas for a trade and business conference.

It is the first time that he has ever stayed in a hotel room and he is somewhat excited about the prospect.

He checks into the hotel and goes up to his room. Five minutes later he calls the desk and says, 'You've given me a room with no exit. How do I leave?'

The desk clerk says, 'Sir, that's absurd. Have you looked for the door?'

The blonde says, 'Well, there's one door that leads to the bathroom. There's a second door that goes into the closet. And there's a door I haven't tried, but it has a "do not disturb" sign on it . . .'

A travelling salesman pulls into a hotel around midnight and asks the clerk for a single room.

As the clerk fills out the paperwork, the man looks around and sees a gorgeous blonde sitting in the lobby.

He tells the clerk to wait while he disappears into the lobby. After a minute he comes back, with the girl on his arm.

'Fancy meeting my wife here,' he says to the clerk. 'Guess I'll need a double room for the night.'

Next morning, he comes to settle his bill and finds the amount to be over $3,000.

'What's the meaning of this?' he yells at the clerk. 'I've only been here one night!'

'Yes,' says the clerk, 'But your wife has been here for three weeks.'

A man who worked at a fire hydrant factory was always late for work.

When confronted by his boss the man explained, 'You can't park anywhere near this place . . .!'

A n office clerk was leaving the office one Friday evening, when she encountered Mr Jones, the Human Resources manager, standing in front of a shredder with a piece of paper in his hand.

'Listen,' said Mr. Jones, 'This is really important and my secretary has already left. Can you show me how to make this thing work?'

'Certainly,' said the clerk. She turned the machine on, inserted the paper and pressed the start button.

'Excellent, excellent!' said Mr Jones as his paper disappeared inside the machine. 'I just need one copy.'

T wo employees for a gas company were at a house call. The younger man noticed the backs of the older man's hands and said, 'Gee, you're old!'

'Yeah, that may be so, but I can still outrun you,' replied the older employee.

'Alright you are on!' said the younger one. 'I challenge you to a foot race to see if you are right.'

With that, they set off running at full speed around the block.

The older man kept up with the younger man around the first corner, started to gain ground on the second corner and by the third corner had shot ahead.

As they approached the last corner, the younger man noticed an elderly woman following them. She is running as fast as her legs can carry her.

Puzzled by this he stops to ask why she is running behind them.

The old woman caught her breath and said, 'Well, you were at my home checking my gas meter and when I saw you running away, I figured I'd better run too!'

A man is hired by the circus to perform a necessary but rather unpleasant task.

His job is to walk behind the elephants in the ring, shovelling their dung up.

After a rather difficult evening at work he goes to the circus cafeteria, sits with the other workers and begins complaining about his work.

'It's just terrible work, walking behind those huge beasts and first dodging, then shovelling their crap,' he says.

'My arms are tired, my shoes and pants are a mess and I stink.'

His friends at work agree, 'Why don't you just quit this miserable job and find something more rewarding to do.

'You must have some skills and talents that you can put to use somewhere else.'

He looks at them, stunned, 'You know, you're probably right, but I just can't give up the glamour of show business!'

A braham wanted a new suit, so he bought a nice piece of cloth and then tried to locate a tailor.

The first tailor he visited looked at the cloth and measured Abraham and then told him the cloth was not enough to make a suit.

Abraham was unhappy with this opinion and sought another tailor.

This tailor measured Abraham and then measured the cloth.

He smiled and said, 'There is enough cloth to make a pair of trousers, a coat and a vest. Come back in a week to pick up your suit.'

After a week Abraham came to take his new suit and noticed the tailor's son wearing trousers made of the same cloth.

Perplexed, he asked, 'Just how could you make a full suit for me and trousers for your son, when the other tailor could not make a suit only?'

'It's very simple,' replied the tailor, 'The other tailor has two sons.'

Andy was being interviewed for a job as signalman on the railways.

The interview was going well, until he was asked what he would do if he realised that two trains were heading for each other on the same track.

Andy thought about it and replied, 'I would switch the points for one of the trains.'

'And what if the lever was broken?' asked the interviewer.

'Then I'd dash down out of the signal box,' said Andy, 'And I'd use the manual lever over there.'

'What if that had been struck by lightning?' countered the interviewer.

'Then,' Andy continued, 'I'd run back into the signal box and phone the next signal box.'

'What if the phone was engaged?'

'Well in that case,' persevered Andy, 'I'd rush down out of the box and use the emergency phone at the level crossing.'

'What if that was vandalised?'

'Oh well, then I'd run into the village and get my Uncle Barry.'

This puzzles the interviewer and so he asks, 'Why would you do that?'

The answer was, 'Because he's never seen a train crash.'

An archaeologist was digging in the Negev Desert in Israel and came upon a casket containing a mummy.

After examining it, he called the curator of a prestigious natural history museum.

'I've just discovered a 3,000-year-old mummy of a man who died of heart failure!' the excited scientist exclaimed.

To which the curator cautiously replied, 'Bring him in. We'll check it out.'

A week later, the amazed curator called the archaeologist. 'You were right about the mummy's age and cause of death. How in the world did you know?'

'Easy. There was a piece of paper in his hand that said, "10,000 Shekels on Goliath".'

There were three boys in the schoolyard bragging about how great their fathers were.

The first one said, 'Well, my father runs the fastest. He can fire an arrow, start to run and he gets there before the arrow.'

The second one snorted, 'Ha! You think that's fast! My father is a hunter. He can shoot his gun and be there before the bullet.'

The third one listened to the other two and shook his head.

He then said, 'You two know nothing about fast. My father is a public servant. He stops working at 4.30 and he is home by 3.45!'

RESUMES, RESUMES . . .

Please call me after 5.30 because I am self-employed and my employer does not know I am looking for another job.

Marital Status: Often. Children: Various.

Minor allergies to house cats and Mongolian sheep.

I procrastinate—especially when the task is unpleasant.
Note: Please don't misconstrue my 14 jobs as 'job-hopping'.
I have never quit a job.

My goal is to be a meteorologist. But since I have no training in meteorology, I suppose I should try stock brokerage.

Personal: I'm married with nine children. I don't require prescription drugs.

I am extremely loyal to my present firm, so please don't let them know of my immediate availability.

Qualifications: I am a man filled with passion and integrity and I can act on short notice. I'm a class act and do not come cheap.

I intentionally omitted my salary history. I've made money and lost money. I've been rich and I've been poor. I prefer being rich.

Wholly responsible for two failed financial institutions.

It is best for employers that I not work with people.

Failed bar exam with relatively high grades.

I have an excellent track record, although I am not a horse.

I have become completely paranoid, trusting completely no one and absolutely nothing.

References: None. I've left a path of destruction behind me

FIVE REASONS FOR LEAVING THE LAST JOB THAT SHOULD NOT BE WRITTEN ON YOUR RESUME

1. Responsibility makes me nervous.
2. They insisted that all employees get to work by 8.45 every morning. Couldn't work under those conditions.

3. Was met with a string of broken promises and lies, as well as cockroaches.
4. I was working for my mum until she decided to move.
5. The company made me a scapegoat—just like my three previous employers.

EXAMPLES AS TO WHY YOU SHOULD ALWAYS PROOFREAD YOUR RESUME

1. I was proud to win the Gregg Typting Award.
2. Work Experience: Dealing with customers' conflicts that arouse.
3. Education: College, August 1880-May 1984.
4. Develop and recommend an annual operating expense fudget.
5. I'm a rabid typist.
6. Instrumental in ruining entire operation for a Mid-west chain operation.
7. Received a plague for Salesperson of the Year.
8. As indicted, I have over five years of analysing investments.

OFFICE OLYMPICS

Pit yourself against your colleagues. See who can score the most points to win office gold.

Points are awarded for each task completed.

One Pointers

Ignore the first five people who say 'good morning' to you.

Run one lap around the office at top speed.

Find the vacuum and start vacuuming around your desk.

Phone someone in the office you barely know, leave your name and say, 'Just called to say I can't talk right now. Bye.'

To signal the end of a conversation, clamp your hands over your ears and grimace.

While riding an elevator, gasp dramatically every time the doors open.

Three Pointers

Babble incoherently at a fellow employee then ask, 'Did you get all that, I don't want to have to repeat it.' Double points if you do this to a manager.

Kneel in front of the water cooler and drink directly from the nozzle.

Shout random numbers while someone is counting.

Lick the shoes of the person sitting next to you.

Take just one bite out of someone's sandwich that is in the fridge.

Five Pointers

At the end of a meeting, suggest that it would be nice to conclude with the singing of the national anthem—three extra points if you actually launch into it yourself.

Eat the unidentifiable substance that has been in the Tupperware container at the back of the fridge for three months.

After every sentence, say 'mun' in a really bad Jamaican accent. As in, 'the report's on your desk, mun'. Keep this up for the day.

In a meeting slap your forehead repeatedly and mutter, 'Shut up, all of you just shut up!'

Come to work in army fatigues and when asked why, say, 'I can't talk about it.'

Speak with an accent (French, German, Porky Pig, etc.) during a very important conference call.

To: All personnel
From: Accounting

It has come to our attention recently that many of you have been turning in timesheets that specify large amounts of 'Miscellaneous Unproductive Time' (Code 5309). However, we need to know exactly what you are doing during your unproductive time.

Attached below is a sheet specifying a tentative extended job code list based on our observations of employee activities.

The list will allow you to specify with a fair amount of precision what you are doing during your unproductive time. Please begin using this job-code list immediately and let us know about any difficulties you encounter.

Thank you,
Accounting

Attached: Extended Job-Code List
            Code and Explanation

5316   Useless Meeting
5317   Obstructing Communications at Meeting
5318   Trying to Sound Knowledgeable While in Meeting
5319   Waiting for Break
5320   Waiting for Lunch
5321   Waiting for End of Day
5322   Vicious Verbal Attacks Directed at Co-worker
5323   Vicious Verbal Attacks Directed at Co-worker while
       Co-worker is Not Present

5393   Covering for Incompetence of Co-worker Friend

5400   Trying to Explain Concept to Co-worker Who is Not
        Interested

5401   Trying to Explain Concept to Co-worker Who is Stupid

5402   Trying to Explain Concept to Co-worker Who Hates You

5481   Buying Snack

5482   Eating Snack

5500   Filling Out Timesheet

5501   Inventing Timesheet Entries

5502   Waiting for Something to Happen

5504   Sleeping

5510   Feeling Bored

5511   Feeling Horny

5600   Complaining About Lousy Job

5601   Complaining About Low Pay

5602   Complaining About Long Hours

5603   Complaining About Co-worker (See Codes #5322 and
        #5323)

5604   Complaining About Boss

5605   Complaining About Personal Problems

5640   Miscellaneous Unproductive Complaining

5701   Not Actually Present At Job

5702   Suffering From Eight-hour Flu

6200   Using Company Resources for Personal Profit

6201   Stealing Company Goods

6203   Using Company Phone to Make Long-Distance Personal
        Calls

6204   Using Company Phone to Make Long-Distance Personal
        Calls to Sell Stolen Company Goods

6205   Hiding from Boss

6206   Gossip

6207   Planning a Social Event (e.g. holiday, wedding, etc.)

6210   Surfing Internet on Non-Job Related Sites

6211   Updating Resume

6212   Faxing Resume to Another Employer/Head-hunter

6213   Out of Office on Interview

6221   Pretending to Work While Boss Is Watching

6350   Playing Pranks on New Co-worker

6603   Writing a Book on Company Time

6611   Staring Into Space

6612   Staring At Computer Screen

6615   Transcendental Meditation

7281   Extended Visit to the Bathroom (at least 10 minutes)

7419   Talking With Miscellaneous Tradespeople on Phone

7425   Talking With Mistress/Toy-Boy on Phone

8000   Recreational Drug Use

8001   Non-recreational Drug Use

8002   Liquid Lunch

8100   Reading Email

WHAT THE COMMENTS ON STAFF EVALUATIONS REALLY MEAN—PART 1

Average: Not too bright.

Exceptionally Well Qualified: Has committed no major
                                    blunders to date.

Active Socially: Drinks Heavily.

Zealous Attitude: Opinionated.

Unlimited Potential: Will stick with us until retirement.

Quick Thinking: Offers plausible excuses for
                                    errors.

Takes Pride in Work:	Conceited.
Takes Advantage of Every Opportunity to Progress:	Buys drinks for superiors.
Approaches Difficult Problems with Logic:	Finds someone else to do the job.
Conscientious and Careful:	Scared.
Meticulous in Attention to Detail:	A nitpicker.
Happy:	Paid too much.
Well Organised:	Looks busy.
Expresses Self Well:	Can string two sentences together.
Spends Extra Hours on the Job:	Miserable home life.

WHAT THE COMMENTS ON STAFF EVALUATIONS REALLY MEAN—PART 2

Demonstrates Qualities of Leadership:	Has a loud voice.
Judgement is Usually Sound:	Lucky.
Maintains Professional Attitude:	A snob.

Keen Sense of Humour:	Knows lots of dirty jokes.
Strong Adherence to Principles:	Stubborn.
Of Great Value to the Organisation:	Turns up to work on time.
Is Unusually Loyal:	Wanted by no-one else.
Alert to Company Developments:	An office gossip.
Hard Worker:	Usually does it the hard way.
Enjoys Job:	Needs more to do.
Consults with Supervisor Often:	Annoying.
Uses Time Effectively:	Clock watcher.
Very Creative:	Finds 22 reasons to do anything except work.
Uses Resources Well:	Delegates everything.
Deserves Promotion:	Create new title to make them feel appreciated.

SAY THAT AGAIN?

HOW? WHAT? WHY?

A graduate with a Science degree asks, 'Why does it work?'
A graduate with an Engineering degree asks, 'How does it work?'

A graduate with an Accounting degree asks, 'How much will it cost?'

A graduate with a Law degree asks, 'Who gave it permission to work?'

A graduate with an Arts degree asks, 'Would you like fries with that?'

A marketing manager got married to a woman who had previously been married eight times.

On his wedding night, his wife informed him that she was still a virgin.

He was flabbergasted that someone who had been married so many times could still be a virgin.

But she sat him down and patiently explained the following,

'My first husband was a sales representative who spent our entire marriage telling me, in grandiose terms, "It's gonna be great!" My second husband was from software services; he was never quite sure how it was supposed to function, but he said he would send me the documentation. My third husband was an accountant. His claimed that he knew how, but he just wasn't sure whether or not it was in his job description. My fourth husband was a teacher and he simply said, "Those who can, do; those who can't, teach." My fifth husband was an engineer. He told me that he understood the basic process but needed three years to research, implement and design a new state-of-the-art method. My sixth husband was a psychiatrist and all he ever wanted to do was talk about it. My seventh husband was a help-desk coordinator and he kept teaching me how to do it myself. My eighth husband was in technical support and he kept saying, "Don't worry, it'll be up any minute now".'

The wife sighed and said sweetly to her new husband, 'Now I am married to you, a man of marketing.'

The husband looked at his wife and simply said, 'I know I have the product, I'm just not sure how to position it.'

The profits of an unlisted company had been in slow decline and so the CEO decided that she should test the competence of her employees.

She wandered out of her office and asked her personal assistant, 'I was just wondering whether you could tell me how much 2 + 2 makes?'

Perplexed, the PA replies, 'I'll get the answer to you in a detailed memo by the end of the day!'

She turns down the corridor to the IT section, 'Hi John! Just a question. Can you tell me how much make 2 + 2?'

John runs Excel and, after several minutes, answers, 'It is 4.00 E+0, but I'm not sure, the support staff should come tomorrow. Will I ask them to check it?'

She heads off to the accountant and asks the same question confident that a man of numbers will be able to answer it.

The accountant looks flustered and says, 'I'm sorry I'm not sure I have all the data that I need to give an accurate reply. I will need to check the accounts, but I can estimate it now between 3.196 . . . and let's say . . . 5.659. But I'll be able to make a much more accurate estimate within two weeks!'

A bit disappointed, she goes to the sales manager:

'Hello Bob, could you tell me how much make 2 + 2?'

'So . . . How much do you think it makes?' is his reply.

'I want your answer.'

'Mmm . . . You don't want to tell me your price. You want me to make an offer. So, let's say 6! No, excuse me, you're not that kind of woman, you know the market. I'll sell it to you for 5.25 and that is the price I'd make for my best friend!'

Exasperated, she goes to the actuary department.

'Can someone please tell me what 2 + 2 makes?'

'Of course,' is the reply. 'How much would you like it to make?'

ANSWER TO THE ULTIMATE QUESTION

Why did the chicken cross the road?

Bill Gates: I have just released the new Chicken Office 2004, which will not only cross roads, but will lay eggs, file your important documents and balance your cheque-book.

Social Worker: It crossed the road to be able to understand both sides.

An actuary: It looked in the file and that's what it did last year.

A consultant: Deregulation of the chicken's side of the road was threatening its dominant market position. The chicken was faced with significant challenges to create and develop the competencies required for the newly competitive market. Our consulting firm, in a partnering relationship with the client, helped the chicken by rethinking its physical distribution strategy and implementation processes. Using the Poultry

Integration Model (PIM), we helped the chicken use its skills, methodologies, knowledge, capital and experiences to align the chicken's people, processes and technology in support of its overall strategy within a Program Management framework. This was conducive towards the creation of a total business integration solution.

SAY WHAT?

Somebody would have been sacked for the following translations . . .

The American Dairy Association's expanded their 'Got Milk?' advertising campaign into Mexico. It was only later that they realised the Spanish translation read, 'Are you lactating?'

Clairol introduced the 'Mist Stick', a curling iron, into Germany only to find out that 'mist' is slang for manure.

A t-shirt maker in Miami printed shirts celebrating the Pope's American visit for the Spanish market. Instead of 'I Saw the Pope' (el Papa), the shirts read 'I Saw the Potato' (la papa).

Pepsi's 'Come Alive With the Pepsi Generation' translated into Chinese meant 'Pepsi Brings Your Ancestors Back From the Grave'.

A chicken company's slogan, 'It takes a strong man to make a tender chicken', was translated into Spanish as 'It takes an aroused man to make a chicken affectionate'.

W hen Parker Pen marketed a ball-point pen in Mexico, its ads were supposed to have read, 'It won't leak in your pocket and embarrass you.' The company thought that the Spanish word 'embarazar' meant to embarrass, but the ad actually read, 'It won't leak in your pocket and make you pregnant'.

SIGNS OF THE TIMES

TEN SIGNS YOU NEED A HOLIDAY . . .

(or 10 signs that perhaps you are not as indispensable as you think!)

1. You get all excited when it's Saturday so you can wear a tracksuit to work.
2. You find you really need Power Point to explain what you do for a living.
3. You lecture the neighbourhood kids selling lemonade on ways to improve their process.
4. You ask your friends to 'think out of the box' when making Friday night plans.
5. You refer to the tomatoes grown in your garden as deliverables.
6. You have dinner from a vending machine and at the most expensive restaurant in town within the same week.
7. You think that 'progressing an action plan' and 'calendarising a project' are acceptable English phrases.
8. You know the people at the airport hotel better than your next door neighbours.
9. You think Einstein would have been more effective had he put his ideas into a matrix.
10. You think a 'half-day' means leaving at 5 o'clock.

THE SEVEN SIGNS YOU ARE BURNT OUT BECAUSE OF WORK

1. Your rubbish bin is your 'in' box.
2. You sleep more at work than at home.
3. You're so tired you now answer the phone, 'Hell.'

4. Visions of the upcoming weekend help you make it through Monday.
5. You think about how relaxing it would be if you were in jail right now.
6. You wake up to discover your bed is on fire, but go back to sleep because you just don't care.
7. Your friend calls to ask how you've been and you immediately scream, 'Get off my back, jerk!'

TEN SIGNS THE COMPANY YOU WORK FOR IS GOING UNDER

1. They start paying everyone in gravel.
2. Company President is now driving a Ford Escort.
3. Dr Jack Kevorkian is hired as part of Human Resources.
4. Your boss casually asks you if you know anything about starting fires.
5. When you say, 'See you tomorrow,' the watchman laughs uncontrollably.
6. The women are suddenly very friendly with the dorky Personnel Manager.
7. The chairman walks by your desk and says, 'Hey, Hey! Easy on the staples!'
8. Annual Company Holiday Bash moved from the Sheraton to Sizzler.
9. Your CEO has a dart board marked with all existing departments in the company.
10. The only office equipment purchased in the last week was four new paper shredders . . .

YOU MUST BE WORKING FOR A HI-TECH COMPANY IF . . .

1. Your relatives describe your job as 'works with computers'.
2. Contractors outnumber permanent staff and are more likely to get long-service awards.

3. Holiday is something you roll over to next year.
4. You're already late on the assignment you just got.
5. Your supervisor doesn't have the ability to do your job.
6. Being sick is defined as you are in hospital—which is okay as long as you have your laptop with you.
7. It's dark when you drive to and from work, even in the summer.
8. You've sat at the same desk for four years and worked for three different companies.
9. Board members' salaries are higher than all the Third World countries' annual budgets combined.
10. There's no money in the budget for the five permanent staff your department is short of, but they can afford four full-time management consultants advising your boss's boss on strategy.

I was sitting in the waiting room of the hospital after my wife had gone into labour and the nurse walked out and said to the man sitting next to me, 'Congratulations sir, you're the new father of twins!'

The man replied, 'How about that, I work for the Double-Mint Chewing Gum company.'

About an hour later, the same nurse entered the waiting room and announced that Mr Smith's wife has just had triplets.

Mr Smith stood up and said, 'Well, how do you like that, I work for the 3M Company.'

The gentleman that was sitting next to me then got up and started to leave.

When I asked him why he was leaving, he remarked, 'I think I need a breath of fresh air, I work for 7-UP.'

E mployer to applicant, 'In this job we need someone who is responsible.'

Applicant, 'I'm the one you want. In my last job, every time anything went wrong, they said I was responsible.'

'**Y**oung man, do you think you can handle a variety of work?'
'I ought to be able to. I've had ten different jobs in four months.'

The local sheriff was looking for a deputy, so Gary went in to try out for the job.

'Okay,' the sheriff drawled, 'Gary, what is 1 and 1?'

'Eleven,' he replied.

The sheriff thought to himself, 'That's not what I meant, but he's right.'

'What two days of the week start with the letter 'T'?' was the next question.

'Today and tomorrow.'

The sheriff was again surprised that Gary supplied a correct answer that he had never thought of himself.

'Now Gary, listen carefully, who killed Abraham Lincoln?'

Gary looked a little surprised himself, then thought really hard for a minute and finally admitted, 'I don't know.'

'Well,' suggested the sheriff, 'Why don't you go home and work on that one for a while?'

So, Gary went home and his wife asked how his interview went.

Gary was exultant. 'It was great! First day on the job and I'm already working on a murder case!'

A man applied for a job as a secret agent.

Together with several other applicants, he was given a sealed envelope and told to take it to the fourth floor.

As soon as the man was alone, he stepped into an empty hallway and opened the envelope.

Inside, a message read, 'You're our kind of person. Report to the fifth floor Personnel Office.'

An applicant was being interviewed for admission to a prominent medical school.

'Tell me,' inquired the interviewer, 'Where do you expect to be ten years from now?'

'Well, let's see,' replied the student. 'It's Wednesday afternoon. I guess I'll be on the golf course by now.'

The navy psychiatrist was interviewing a potential sailor.

To check on the young man's response to trouble, the psychiatrist asked, 'What would you do if you looked out of that window right now and saw a battleship coming down the street?'

The young sailor said, 'I'd grab a torpedo and sink it.'

'Where would you get the torpedo?'

'The same place you got your battleship!'

A HR Manager to job candidate, 'I see you've had no computer training. Although that qualifies you for upper management, it means you're under-qualified for our entry level positions.'

Several weeks after a young man had been hired, he was called into the personnel manager's office.

'What is the meaning of this?' the manager asked. 'When you applied for the job, you told us you had five years' experience.

'Now we discover this is the first job you've ever had.'

'Well,' the young man said, 'In your ad you said you wanted somebody with imagination.'

STUCK ON THE NET

YOU KNOW YOU ARE AN INTERNET JUNKIE WHEN . . .

- When asked to give your home address, your answer begins with http://
- Instead of calling you to dinner, your spouse sends e-mail.
- You know the difference between Java and Javascript.
- In order to watch CNN you move to www.cnn.com.
- You find yourself typing 'com' after every full stop when using a word processor.com.
- You can perfectly imitate the sound pattern of your modem connecting to your ISP.
- You are told about a new program and you are disappointed to find that it is a TV program.
- You wake up at 3 am to go to the bathroom and stop to check your email on the way back to bed.

SIGNS THAT YOUR INTERNET CONNECTION IS A LITTLE SLOW

Text on web pages display as Morse Code.

Your credit card expires while ordering on-line.

Playboy web site exhibits 'Playmate of the Year' . . . for 1989.

You're still in the middle of down-loading that popular new game, 'Frogger'.

You receive e-mails with stamps on them.

You click the 'Send' button, a little door opens on the side of your monitor and a pigeon flies out.

SIGNS THAT YOU'VE OVERDOSED ON THE WORLD WIDE WEB

Your bookmark takes 15 minutes to scroll from top to bottom.

Your pick up line is, 'So, what's your homepage address?'

You felt driven to consult the 'Cool Page of the Day' on your wedding day.

When you read a magazine, you have an irresistible urge to click on the underlined passages.

Your dog has his own web-page.

So does your hamster.

TAXING TIMES

The tax advisor had just read the story of Cinderella to his four-year-old daughter for the first time.

The little girl was fascinated by the story, especially the part where the pumpkin turns into a golden coach.

Suddenly she asks, 'Daddy, when the pumpkin turned into a golden coach, would that be classed as income or a long-term capital gain?'

What is the difference between tax avoidance and tax evasion? The jail walls.

'How have you managed to buy such a luxurious villa while your income is so low?' asked the tax auditor.

'Well,' the taxpayer answered, 'While fishing last summer I caught a large golden fish. When I took it off the hook, the fish opened his mouth and said, "I am a magical fish. Throw me back to the sea and I'll give you the most luxurious villa you have ever seen." I threw the fish back to the sea and got the villa.'

'How can you prove such an unbelievable story?'

'Well, you can see the villa, can't you?'

The local bar was so sure that its bartender was the strongest man around that they offered a standing $1000 bet—the bartender would squeeze a lemon until all the juice ran into a glass and hand the lemon to a patron. Anyone who could squeeze one more drop of juice out would win the money.

Many people had tried over time but nobody could do it.

One day this scrawny little man came into the bar, wearing thick glasses and a polyester suit and said in a tiny squeaky voice, 'I'd like to try the bet.'

After the laughter had died down, the bartender grabbed a lemon and squeezed away. Then he handed the wrinkled remains of the rind to the little man.

The crowd's laughter turned to total silence as the man clenched his fist around the lemon and six drops fell into the glass.

As the crowd cheered, the bartender paid the $1000 and asked the little man 'What do you do for a living? Are you a lumberjack, a weight-lifter or what?'

The man replied, 'I work for the tax department.'

A man, about to enter hospital, saw two white coated doctors searching through the flower beds.

'Excuse me,' he said, 'Have you lost something?'

'No,' replied one of the doctors, 'We're doing a heart transplant for an income-tax inspector and want to find a suitable stone.'

A man takes a balloon ride at a local country fair. A fierce wind suddenly kicks up, causing the balloon to violently leave the fair and carry its occupant out into the countryside.

The man has no idea where he is, so he goes down to five metres above ground and asks a passer-by, 'Excuse me, sir, can you tell me where I am?'

Eyeing the man in the balloon the passer-by says, 'You are in a red balloon, five metres above ground.'

The balloon's unhappy resident replied, 'You must be a Microsoft tutorial writer.'

'How could you possibly know that?' asked the passer-by.

'Because your answer is technically correct but absolutely useless and the fact is I am still lost.'

'Then you must be in management,' said the passer-by.

'That's right! How did you know?'

'You have such a good view from where you are, yet you don't know where you are nor where you are going. The fact is you are in the exact same position you were in before we met, but now your problem is somehow my fault!'

An economist and an accountant are walking beside a pond when they come across a frog.

The economist says, 'If you eat the frog I'll give you $20,000!'

Adding up his figures the accountant quickly agrees and chokes down the live frog. The economist hands over a suitcase of cash.

They continue walking around the pond when they encounter another frog. Always up for some fun the accountant says, 'If you eat this frog I'll give you $20,000.'

So the economist eats the frog and the accountant hands the suitcase back to him.

After a few minutes of thought the accountant says, 'Look we both have the same amount of money we had before, but we both ate frogs. I don't see us being better off.'

The economist, 'Well, that's true, but you overlooked the fact that we've just been involved in $40,000 worth of trade.'

A man with a wooden leg wanted to buy fire insurance for his leg.

The first actuary quoted an annual premium of $500, estimating that the leg would burn once in 20 years and the value of the leg is $10,000.

The second actuary quoted an annual premium of $50.

When the second actuary was asked how he arrived at such a small figure, he replied, 'I have this situation in the fire schedule rating table. The object is a wooden structure with an upper sprinkler, isn't it?'

What's the difference between an insurance company actuary and a mafia actuary?

An insurance company actuary can tell you how many people will die this year, a mafia actuary can name them.

An actuary and a farmer were travelling by train. When they passed a flock of sheep in a meadow, the actuary said, 'There are 1248 sheep out there.'

The farmer replied, 'Amazing. By chance, I know the owner and the figure is absolutely correct. How did you count them so quickly?'

The actuary answered, 'Easy, I just counted the number of legs and divided by four.'

A doctor, a lawyer and a manager were discussing the relative merits of having a wife or a mistress.

The lawyer says, 'For sure, a mistress is better. If you have a wife and want a divorce, it causes all sorts of legal problems.'

The doctor says, 'It's better to have a wife because the sense of security lowers your stress and is good for your health.'

The manager says, 'You're both wrong. It's best to have both so that when the wife thinks you're with the mistress and the mistress thinks you're with your wife, you can go to the office and do some work.'

The president of a large corporation opened his directors meeting by announcing, 'All those who are opposed to the plan I am about to propose will reply by saying, "I resign".'

TRUE TRIUMVIRATE

By three measures a manager is known:

1. The thickness of the carpet in his office.

2. The area of his desk.
3. The volume of his car's engine.

FIVE RULES TO BEING A SUCCESSFUL COMMITTEE MEMBER

1. Never arrive on time.
2. Don't say anything until the meeting is half over.
3. Be as vague as possible.
4. When in doubt, suggest that a subcommittee be appointed.
5. Be the first to move for adjournment; this will make you popular—it's what everyone is waiting for.

Committee—a group of men who individually can do nothing but as a group decide that nothing can be done.

There was a glass of water on the table . . .
One man says, 'It's half full.' He is an optimist.
Second man says, 'It's half empty.' He is a pessimist.
Third man says, 'It's twice too big.' He is a management consultant.

A CONSULTANT IS . . .

Someone who takes the watch off your wrist and tells you the time.

A man who knows 99 ways to make love, but doesn't know any women.

Someone who is called in at the last moment and paid enormous amounts of money to assign the blame.

MORE TRUISMS

- It takes two things to be a consultant—grey hair and haemorrhoids. The grey hair makes you look distinguished and the haemorrhoids make you look concerned.
- In case of doubt, make it sound convincing.
- An expert is one who knows more and more about less and less, until he knows absolutely everything about nothing.
- To spot the expert, pick the one who predicts the job will take the longest and cost the most.
- After all is said and done, a hell of a lot more is said than done.
- If you consult enough experts, you can confirm any opinion.

Three businessmen are fishing in the Caribbean. The first says, 'I had a terrible fire; I lost everything. Now the insurance company is paying for everything and that's why I'm here.'

The second businessman says, 'I had a terrible explosion, I lost everything. Now the insurance company is paying for everything and that's why I'm here.'

The last says, 'What a coincidence. I had a terrible flood, I lost everything. Now the insurance company is paying for everything and that's why I'm here.'

The other guys turned to him with confusion and asked, 'Flood? How do you start a flood?'

Life insurance agent to would-be client: 'Don't let me frighten you into a hasty decision. Sleep on it tonight. If you wake in the morning, give me a call then and let me know.'

'You ought to feel highly honoured,' said the businessman to the life insurance agent, 'so far today I have had my secretary turn away seven insurance agents.'

'Yes, I know,' replied the agent, 'I'm them.'

A keen country lad applied for a salesman's job at a city department store. At the end of his first day on the job his boss fronted up and asked, 'How many sales did you make today?'

'One,' said the young salesman.

'Only one,' blurted the boss, 'Most of my staff make 20 or 30 sales a day. How much was the sale worth?'

'100,000 dollars,' said the young man.

'How did you manage that?' asked the flabbergasted boss.

'Well,' said the salesman 'This man came in and I sold him a small fish hook, then a medium hook and finally a really large hook. Then I sold him a small fishing line, a medium one and a huge big one. I asked him where he was going fishing and he said down the coast. I said he would probably need a boat, so I took him down to the boat department and sold him that 20 foot schooner with the twin engines. Then he said his Volkswagen probably wouldn't be able to pull it, so I took him to the car department and sold him the new Deluxe Cruiser.'

The boss took two steps back and asked in astonishment, 'You sold all that to a guy who came in for a fish hook?'

'Not exactly,' answered the salesman, 'He actually came in to buy a box of tampons for his wife and I said to him, 'Your weekend's shot, you may as well go fishing.'

A salesman walking along the beach found a bottle. When he rubbed it, lo and behold, a genie appeared.

'I will grant you three wishes,' announced the genie. 'But since Satan still hates me, for every wish you make, your rival gets the wish as well—only double.'

The salesman thought about this for a while. 'For my first wish, I would like ten million dollars,' he announced.

Instantly the genie gave him a Swiss bank account number and assured the man that $10,000,000 had been deposited. 'But your rival has just received $20,000,000,' the genie said.

'I've always wanted a Ferrari,' the salesman said.

A red Ferrari appeared.

'But your rival has just received two Ferraris,' the genie said. 'And what is your last wish?'

'Well,' said the salesman, 'I've always wanted to donate a kidney for transplant.'

When a young salesman met his untimely end, he was informed that he had a choice about where he would spend his eternity, heaven or hell. He was allowed to visit both places and then make his decision afterwards.

'I'll see heaven first,' said the salesman and an angel led him through the gates on a private tour.

Inside it was very peaceful and serene. All the people there were playing harps and eating grapes. It looked very nice, but the salesman was not about to make a decision without visiting hell.

'Can I see hell now?' he asked.

The angel pointed him to the elevator and he went down to the basement where he was greeted by one of Satan's loyal followers.

For the next half hour the salesman was led through a tour of what appeared to be the best night clubs he'd ever seen. People were partying loudly, drinking, flirting and having a 'hell' of a time.

When the tour ended, he was sent back up where the angel

asked him if he had reached a final decision.

'Yes, I have,' he replied. 'As great as heaven looks and all, I have to admit that hell was more my kind of place. I've decided to spend my eternity down there.'

The salesman was sent to hell. He was immediately thrown into a cave and chained to a wall where he was subjected to various tortures.

'When I came down here for the tour,' he yelled with anger and pain, 'I was shown a whole bunch of bars and parties and other great stuff! What happened?'

The Devil replied, 'Oh, that! That was just the sales demo.'

Two shoe salespeople were sent to Africa to open up new markets.

Three days after arriving, one salesperson called the office and said, 'I'm returning on the next flight. Can't sell shoes here. Everybody goes barefoot.'

At the same time the other salesperson sent an email to the factory, saying 'The prospects are unlimited. Nobody wears shoes here!'

The Devil tells a salesman, 'Look, I can make you richer, more famous and more successful than any salesman alive. In fact, I can make you the greatest salesman that ever lived.'

'Well,' says the salesman, 'What do I have to do in return?'

The Devil smiles, 'Well, of course you have to give me your soul,' he says, 'But you also have to give me the souls of your children, the souls of your children's children and, as a matter of fact, you have to give me the souls of all your descendants throughout eternity.'

'Wait a minute,' the salesman says cautiously, 'What's the catch?'

A merchant teaches his son the secrets of the trade.
'When you charge a customer $100 and he pays you by mistake $200, you have an ethical dilemma—should you tell your partner?'

Jones applied to a debt collecting agency for a job even though he had no experience.

He was very intense and so the manager gave him a tough account with the promise that if he collected it, he'd get the job.

Two hours later, Jones came back with the entire amount.

'Amazing!' the manager said. 'How did you do it?'

'Easy,' Jones replied. 'I told him if he didn't pay up, I'd tell all his other creditors he paid us.'

TECHNICIANS, TECHNICIANS

The son of a technician asks his father, 'Daddy, why does the sun rise in the east and go down at the west?'

The technician answers immediately, 'If it ain't broke, don't fix it.'

'And why it is so hot today?' the kid continues to ask.

'If it's bothering you, turn it off and then turn on again'.

During the French Revolution a priest, a lawyer and a technician were lined up at the guillotine to be beheaded. They were given the choice to look up or to look face down in the guillotine.

The priest said, 'Well, heaven is up, so I'll look up, so I can see where I'm going.'

They placed the priest in the guillotine facing up and released the blade.

The blade stopped just inches from the priest, so they let him go, thinking it was a miracle.

The lawyer thought, 'Well if it worked for the priest, it might work for me,' so they placed him in the guillotine looking up.

They released the blade and it stopped just inches from the lawyer.

He stood up and claimed he couldn't be executed twice for the same crime and so walked free.

The technician thought, 'Well why not?'

They put him in the guillotine looking up and the technician said, 'Wait a minute! If you swap the red and the blue wires over, you might make this thing work . . .'

A communication technician drafted by the army was at a firing range.

At the range he was given a rifle and 50 rounds. He began firing but after several shots it was reported that all his attempts had completely missed the target.

The technician looked at his weapon and then at the target.

He looked at the weapon again and then at the target again.

He then put his finger over the end of the rifle barrel and squeezed the trigger with his other hand.

The end of his finger was blown off, whereupon he yelled towards the target area, 'It's leaving here just fine, the trouble must be at your end!'

Four surgeons were taking a coffee break and were discussing their work.

The first said, 'I think accountants are the easiest to operate on. You open them up and everything inside is numbered.'

The second said, 'I think librarians are the easiest to operate on.

You open them up and everything inside is in alphabetical order.'

The third said, 'I like to operate on electricians. You open them up and everything inside is colour-coded.'

The fourth surgeon said, 'I like technicians . . . they always understand when you have a few parts left over at the end . . .'

A salesman, an engineer and a technician are driving in a car when, just outside of town, they get a flat tyre. The three of them get out of the car and scratch their heads.

The salesman says, 'Maybe I should walk into town and get us a new tyre. I know that I can bargain with the man at the parts store and get us a great deal.'

The engineer stops him, saying, 'No, before you do that, we'll have to do some computations, find the grade of the road, the asphalt temperature and the average rate of speed we will be travelling to know what kind of tyre you should buy.'

The technician laughs and shakes his head. 'No, no, no! What's wrong with you guys? Hell, we have a spare tyre in the boot—now all we have to do is start swapping tyres until we find the flat one!'

THE BUSINESS OF IT

Jack was a COBOL programmer in the late 1990s.
After years of being taken for granted and treated as a technological dinosaur by all the other programmers and website developers he became a private consultant specialising in Year 2000 conversions.

Several years of this relentless, mind-numbing compliance work took its toll on Jack.

He began having anxiety dreams about the Year 2000.

All he could think about was how he could avoid the Year 2000 altogether.

Jack decided to contact a company that specialised in cryogenics. He asked to have himself frozen until January 1, 2001.

He would miss out entirely on the Year 2000 and any resulting computer failures. Once thawed, he would be able to happily continue with his life without the spectre of the Year 2000 hanging over him.

So in December 1999 his heart was slowed to several beats a minute, he was put into his cryogenic receptacle, the technicians set his revival date and Jack hibernated.

The next thing that Jack knew was an enormous and very modern room filled with excited people.

They were all shouting 'I can't believe it!', 'It's a miracle' and 'He's alive!'

Neither could Jack—he had missed out on the Year 2000 completely! He wanted to know whether the Y2K problem had been as catastrophic as predicted.

A doctor stepped forward and gently explained that it was not 2001 as Jack thought. There had been a problem with the programming of the timer on Jack's cryogenic receptacle as it hadn't been Year 2000 compliant and it was actually eight thousand years later! Technology had advanced to such a degree that everyone had virtual reality interfaces that allowed them to contact anyone else on the planet.

'That sounds terrific,' said Jack. 'But I'm curious. Why is everybody so interested in me?'

'Well,' said the spokesman. 'It is 9999 and the year 10,000 is just around the corner. It says in your files that you know COBOL.'

How do you keep a programmer in the shower all day? Give him a bottle of shampoo that says 'Lather, rinse, repeat.'

A man lies back and lights up a post-coital cigarette. His lover turns to him and says, 'Can't you see the warning written on the cigarette packet, smoking is harmful to your health!'

'Darling,' he says 'I'm a programmer. We don't worry about warnings, we only worry about errors.'

THE PROGRAMMERS' CHEER

Shift to the left, shift to the right! Pop up, push down, byte, byte, byte!

One programmer asked another, 'Have you heard about the object-oriented way to become wealthy?'
'No,' the second replied.
'Inheritance.'

THE IT GUIDE TO REALITY

If you can touch it and you can see it, it's real.

If you can touch it but you can't see it, it's transparent.

If you can't touch it but you can see it, it's virtual.

If you can't touch it and you can't see it, it's gone.

If you can pick it up, it's a personal computer.

If you can't pick it up but you can push it over, it's a minicomputer.

But when you can't pick it up or knock it over, it's a mainframe.

In C we had to code our own bugs. In C++ we can inherit them. C gives you enough rope to hang yourself. C++ also gives you the tree object to tie it to.

With C you can shoot yourself in the leg. With C++ you can reuse the bullet.

Why did all Pascal programmers ask to live in Atlantis? Because it is below C level.

There are three kinds of lies: lies, damned lies and benchmarks.

SOFTWARE DEVELOPMENT CYCLE

1. Programmer produces code he believes is bug-free.
2. Product is tested. Twenty bugs are found.
3. Programmer fixes 10 of the bugs and explains to the testing department that the other 10 aren't really bugs.
4. Testing department finds that five of the fixes didn't work and discovers 15 new bugs.
5. Repeat three times steps 3 and 4.
6. Due to marketing pressure and an extremely premature product announcement based on overly optimistic programming schedule, the product is released.
7. Users find 137 new bugs.

8. Original programmer, having cashed his royalty cheque, is nowhere to be found.
9. Newly assembled programming team fixes almost all of the 137 bugs, but introduce 456 new ones.
10. Company is bought in a hostile takeover by competitor using profits from their latest release, which had 783 bugs.
11. New CEO is bought in by board of directors. He hires a programmer to redo program from scratch.
12. Programmer produces code he believes is bug-free ...

A programmer was walking along the beach when he found a lamp.

Upon rubbing the lamp a genie appeared who proclaimed, 'I am the most powerful genie in the world. I can grant you any wish you want, but only one wish.'

The programmer pulled out a map of the Middle East and said, 'I'd like there to be a just and lasting peace among these people.'

The genie responded, 'Gee, I don't know. Those people have been fighting since the beginning of time. I can do just about anything, but this is beyond my limits.'

The programmer then said, 'Well, I am a programmer and my programs have a lot of users. Please make all the users satisfied with my programs.'

The Genie replied, 'Uh, let me see that map again.'

There was a new super computer that took up a whole room. It was so quick and powerful that its makers claimed that it knew absolutely everything.

A sceptical man, trying to trick the computer, asked, 'Where is my father?'

The computer cogitated for a short while and then flashed up on its screen, 'Your father is fishing in Michigan.'

The man snorted and said triumphantly, 'You see? I knew this was nonsense. My father has been dead for 20 years.'

'No,' replied the super computer immediately. 'Your mother's husband has been dead for 20 years. Your father just landed a three pound trout.'

The programmer to his son, 'Here, I brought you a new basketball.'
'Thank you, Daddy, but where is the user's guide?'

THE PROBLEM WITH ...

The problem with physicists is that they tend to cheat in order to get results.

The problem with mathematicians is that they tend to work on toy problems in order to get results.

The problem with program verifiers is that they tend to cheat at toy problems in order to get results.

A software verifier read in the bible that God protects all fools and decided to test it empirically.

He jumped out of the 2nd floor window and broke a leg.

As he lay there writhing in pain he happily thought, 'I never really considered myself a fool, but I never knew I was that clever!'

IN THE BEGINNING ...

In the beginning God created the Bit and the Byte. And from those he created the Word.

And there were two Bytes in the Word; and nothing else existed.

And God separated the One from the Zero; and he saw it was good.

And God said—Let the Data be; and so it happened.

And God said—Let the Data go to their proper places. And he created floppy disks and hard disks and compact disks.

And God said—Let the computers be, so there would be a place to put floppy disks and hard disks and compact disks. Thus God created computers and called them hardware.

And there was no Software yet. But God created programs; small and big. And told them—Go and multiply yourselves and fill all the Memory.

And God said, I will create the Programmer; and the Programmer will make new programs and govern over the computers and programs and Data.

And God created the Programmer; and put him at Data Centre.

And God showed the Programmer the Catalogue Tree and said, You can use all the volumes and sub-volumes but do not use Windows.

And God said—It is not good for the programmer to be alone. So He took a bone from the Programmer's body and created a creature that would look up at the Programmer; and admire the Programmer; and love the things the Programmer does; and God called the creature: the User.

And the Programmer and the User were left under the naked DOS and it was good.

But Bill was smarter than all the other creatures of God. And Bill said to the User—Did God really tell you not to run any programs?

And the User answered—God told us that we can use every program and every piece of Data but told us not to run Windows or we will die.

And Bill said to the User—How can you talk about something you did not even try? The moment you run Windows you will become equal to God. You will be able to create anything you like by a simple click of your mouse.

And the User saw that the fruits of the Windows were nicer and easier to use. And the User saw that any knowledge was useless—since Windows could replace it.

So the User installed the Windows on his computer; and said to the Programmer that it was good.

And the Programmer immediately started to look for new drivers. And God asked him—What are you looking for? And the Programmer answered—I am looking for new drivers because I can not find them in the DOS. And God said—Who told you you need drivers? Did you run Windows? And the Programmer said—It was Bill who told us to!

And God said to Bill—Because of what you did you will be hated by all the creatures. And the User will always be unhappy with you. And you will always sell Windows.

And God said to the User—Because of what you did, the Windows will disappoint you and eat up all your Resources; and you will have to use lousy programs; and you will always rely on the Programmers' help.

And God said to the Programmer—Because you listened to the User you will never be happy. All your programs will have errors and you will have to fix them and fix them to the end of time.

And God threw them out of the Data Centre and locked the door and secured it with a password.

COMPUTER INDUSTRY ACRONYMS

CD-ROM:	Consumer Device, Rendered Obsolete in Months
ISDN:	It Still Does Nothing
MIPS:	Meaningless Indication of Processor Speed
DOS:	Defunct Operating System
WINDOWS:	Will Install Needless Data On Whole System
OS/2:	Obsolete Soon, Too
PnP:	Plug and Pray
APPLE:	Arrogance Produces Profit-Losing Entity
IBM:	I Blame Microsoft
MICROSOFT:	Most Intelligent Customers Realise Our Software Only Fools Teenagers
COBOL:	Completely Obsolete Business Oriented Language
MACINTOSH:	Most Applications Crash; If Not, The Operating System Hangs

THE EIGHT LAWS OF COMPUTING

1. When you get to the point where you really understand your computer, it's probably obsolete.
2. The first place to look for information is in the section of the manual where you least expect to find it.
3. When the going gets tough, the tough upgrade.
4. For every action, there is an equal and opposite malfunction.
5. He who laughs last probably made a back-up.
6. A complex system that does not work is invariably found to have evolved from a simpler system that worked just fine.

7. The number one cause of computer problems is computer solutions.
8. A computer program will always do what you tell it to do, but rarely what you want it to do.

THE POSTIE

A woman went to the Post Office to buy stamps for her Christmas cards.

'What denomination?' asked the clerk.

'Oh, good heavens! Have we come to this?' said the woman. 'Well, give me 30 Catholic, 10 Baptist ones, 20 Lutheran and 40 Presbyterian.'

A Post Office worker at the main sorting office finds an unstamped, hand-written envelope addressed to God.

He opens it and discovers it is from an elderly lady, distressed because some thief robbed her of 100 dollars. It says she will be cold and hungry for the rest of the month if she doesn't receive some divine intervention.

The worker is moved and organises a collection amongst the other postal workers, who dig deep and come up with 96 dollars. They send it by special courier that same morning.

A week later, the same postal worker recognises the same hand-writing on another envelope addressed to God.

He opens it and reads,

'Dear God, Thank you for the 100 dollars. This month would have been so bleak otherwise. P.S. It was four dollars short but that was probably those thieving bastards at the Post Office.'

The neighbourhood postman was retiring after 30 years. On his last day of delivering mail, all of the people on his route left him something in the mail box in honour of his retirement.

Some left money, some left small gifts and some met him at the door and invited him in for a drink.

As he was putting the mail in the mailbox of the last house, the door opened and the woman of the house stood there in beautiful lingerie.

She invited him inside and led him upstairs where she made passionate love to him.

After their lovemaking she took him downstairs where she had prepared an exquisite dinner for him.

Halfway through the course he found a dollar bill under his plate. Confused he asked the woman why it was there.

She explained, 'When I called my husband to ask him what we should give you for your retirement, he said, 'Screw him, give him a dollar.' Dinner was my idea.'

THE PSYCHOLOGY OF IT ALL

A psychiatrist was conducting a group therapy session with four young mothers and their small children.

'You all have obsessions,' he observed.

To the first mother he said, 'You are obsessed with eating. You even named your daughter Candy.'

He turned to the second mum. 'Your obsession is money. Again, it manifests itself in your child's name, Penny.'

He turned to the third mum. 'Your obsession is alcohol and your child's name is Brandy.'

At this point, the fourth mother got up, took her little boy by the hand and whispered, 'Come on, Dick, let's go home.'

Two elderly couples were enjoying friendly conversation when one of the men asked the other, 'Fred, how was the memory clinic you went to last month?'

'Outstanding,' Fred replied. 'They taught us all the latest psychological techniques—visualisation, association—it has made a huge difference for me.'

'That's great! What was the name of the clinic?'

Fred went blank. He thought and thought, but couldn't remember. Then a smile broke across his face and he asked, 'What do you call that red flower with the long stem and thorns?'

'You mean a rose?'

'Yes, that's it!' He turned to his wife, 'Rose, what was the name of that clinic?'

Two psychologists meet at their twentieth college reunion. One of them looks like he just graduated, while the other psychologist looks old, worried and withered.

The older looking one asks the other, 'What's your secret? Listening to other people's problems every day, all day long, for years on end, has made an old man of me.'

The younger looking one replies, 'Who listens?'

Patient:	Doctor, my wife thinks I'm crazy because I like sausages.
Psychiatrist:	Nonsense! I like sausages too.
Patient:	Good, you should come and see my collection. I've got hundreds of them.

A man goes to a psychologist and says, 'Doctor I've got a real problem, I can't stop thinking about sex.'

The psychologist nods sagely and pulls out his book of ink blots.

'Tell me what you can see in this picture,' he asks.

The man turns the picture upside down and says, 'That's a man and a woman on a bed making love.'

'Very interesting,' the psychologist says.

He then shows him the next ink blot, 'And what is this a picture of?'

The man looks and turns it sideways and says, 'That's a man and a woman on a bed making love.'

'Hmmm', the psychologist shows the man the third ink blot.

The patient again turns it in all directions and replies, 'That's a man and a woman on a bed making love.'

The psychologist states, 'Well, yes, you do seem to be obsessed with sex.'

'Me?' demands the patient. 'You're the one who keeps showing me the dirty pictures!'